SMOKED BEERS

SMOKED BEERS

History, Brewing Techniques, Recipes

Ray Daniels and Geoffrey Larson

Classic Beer Style Series No. 18

Brewers Publications
a division of the Brewers Association
Boulder, Colorado

The Classic Beer Style Series is devoted to offering in-depth information on world-class styles by exploring their history, flavor profiles, brewing methods, recipes, and ingredients.

Other Books in the Classic Beer Style Series

Kölsch
Altbier
Barley Wine
Stout
Bock
Scotch Ale
German Wheat Beer
Belgian Ale
Porter
Oktoberfest, Vienna, Märzen
Continental Pilsener
Brown Ale
Mild Ale
Pale Ale
Bavarian Helles

Contents

Acknowledgments

No worthwhile book on the subject of brewing can be completed without input from many sources. As a result, our work on this volume brought us into contact with many individuals who imparted their wisdom and helped to point us in the right direction.

The first person we must mention is Geoff's wife, Marcy Larson. She is truly the third author of this book, having provided immeasurable help from beginning to end. She was present for much of the field research in Europe, helping with logistics and contributing to our thoughts through her own observations and our many discussions over smoked beers. For Geoff, she has helped directly in compiling data, serving as a sounding board and suggesting enhancements to drafts of the text. Without her contributions, this book would lack many of its essential elements.

Our second mention must go to Sabine Weyermann and her husband Thomas Kraus-Weyermann. This couple represents the third-generation of distinguished Bamberg maltsters. As makers of beechwood-smoked malt, they help to preserve the tradition of rauchbier amongst Bamberg-area brewers while spreading the gospel of smoke-flavored beers to brewers around the world. Through their hospitality and their many generous introductions, we managed to garner a detailed understanding of the malting and brewing processes that produce the classic Bamberg rauchbier. During our visits, they shared their home, their knowledge and their library so that we could get the information needed to make this book a reality.

Other maltsters who contributed to this book is Bob McWilliam and Lorne Watson of Bairds Malt Limited in Arbroath, Scotland. They provided Geoff with a day-long tour of the peated malt production and laboratory facility. Their experience with peated malt gave us insights that would not otherwise have been possible.

Of course many brewers shared their wisdom with us, often as part of an in-depth tour of their facilities. Herr Martin Knob, head brewer at Schlenkerla, generously shared his time with us on more than one occasion as he led us through the fascinating brewery that produces this classic beer. At Spezial, owner and brewmaster Christian Merz indulged us in a detailed discussion of his operation and its history. Georg & Margareta Wörner from Bamberg's Kaiserdom brewery hosted us at their beautiful restaurants while filling us in on the details of their export rauchbier and also the domestically distributed black beer that contains smoked malt. At the smaller breweries where we showed up unannounced, the owners were only too happy to show off their facilities and chat with Americans interested in smoked beer. We found a warm reception at Brauerei Kraus, Brauerei Barnikel and especially Brauerei Fischer. At Drei Kronen Gasthof, owner Hans-Ludwig Straub not only talked with us at length, but welcomed Geoff back the next day to participate in the brewing. The Gewalt family was kind enough to show Ray their maltings in Erlangen as well as their American-style Hausbrauerei Steinbach-Bräu.

One of the most interesting events of Ray's time in Bamberg was making a connection that led him to a treasure trove of historical brewing books at Weihenstephan. There Martin Zarnkow hosted him for a day of research in German brewing texts that dated back to 1585 and also treated him to a taste of a wonderful smoked doppelbock.

During Geoff's research, he was assisted by the library staff of the University of California, Davis, during a three day beer research foray. Axel Borg and the rest of the reference staff that helped him navigate the recently acquired Hurty Peck collection. Their comments, help and passion for beverage literature guided Geoff into a better understanding of the past.

Acknowledgments

We want to thank all the breweries that responded to our requests for information about their beers with smoke flavor. We apologize that we could not profile every beer with equal emphasis as each and every one of you are pioneers in this modern rarity which at one time was the everyday expectation. The intended thrust of the book was more of an overview than a guide to all of the existing beers made with smoke. For any omissions, we apologize as they certainly were not intended.

Geoff owes a debt of gratitude to everyone at Alaskan Brewing Company who allowed him to put time into this book by shouldering additional work burdens that fell to them as a result. Ray owes great thanks to his family for the time spent on this project and also to Stephanie Johnson and Amahl Turczyn at the Association of Brewers for keeping *Zymurgy* and *The New Brewer* on track while he "checked out" for several weeks to work on this ancillary project.

We owe a special debt of thanks to Greg Noonan. The first smoked beer that Ray ever remembers drinking was one of Greg's lightly peated Wee Heavys served up during the 1991 American Homebrewers Conference in Manchester, NH. Were it not for that tasty introduction, Ray might never have developed his interest in this subject. Greg also took Geoff through New England during his research travels and talked with him about his experiences making smoked beers. Finally, he served as the technical editor for this text – a fact that allowed both of us to sleep more soundly as this project headed toward its final days.

We would like to acknowledge Michael Jackson and the entire writing community who are simultaneously helping to document and keep alive our brewing heritage. The beer journalism community continues to foster and educate the public as to beer's diversity during a time that this industry is being pressured into mergers and consolidations, jeopardizing this diversity.

Of course no book would be possible without the support of the publishing staff at the Association of Brewers. We extend a special thanks to our publisher, Toni Knapp and our copyeditor Mary Eberle. Also we appreciate the efforts of Tyra Segars and the Graphics Department who created the "package" that you now hold in your hands.

Introduction

When I was asked to help write a book about smoke-flavored beers with Ray Daniels, I jumped at the opportunity. I have had a personal interest in smoke since as early as I could reach the forbidden jar of matches. I earned the nickname *Pyro* when I worked on high school chemistry projects for fun after class identifying combustion distillates. I love the outdoors where the campfire is a central part of the outing, providing heat and light and is used for cooking. The smell of campfire smoke ends up on everything you wear, but that doesn't matter as it smells great! Here in Alaska, wood fires are a part of what I consider the good life. Even the foods we eat have a lot of smoke character, especially the smoked salmon. Smoke has been associated with a lot of enjoyment in my life. Working on a book on smoke-flavored beers sounded like just too much fun to pass up.

While smoked beer is considered a classic beer style for the purposes of this book, it actually crosses many classic beer style boundaries. Smoked flavor in beer has no single origin. There was a time, historically, when almost all beer styles had some smoked character in them as the drying of malt was usually over a directly fired heat source. With the development of more sophisticated heat sources, smoke generation could be greatly reduced or even eliminated. Paradoxically, smoked beer became a separate style when beer was routinely made without smoked flavor. One could say that the process of smoked beers becoming a classic style began with the demise of smoke flavor in beer.

I had a lot of fun early on in the writing of this book as the first mission Ray and I had was to investigate the chemistry of smoke—a subject I had a long association with stemming from high school. As luck would have it, Ray has a degree in biochemistry, which along with my chemical engineering background soon started to make this book look more like a graduate chemistry course than anything a beer enthusiast would want to read. We both wised up, as we know that chemistry is not the subject to bring up at a party if you want people to stay awake for very long.

The investigation then turned to other breweries where I met a lot of great people in the same profession as I. We visited both old and new breweries producing smoked beers, wherever we could find them. Some were new brewpubs in the United States producing smoked beers to augment their food entrees; others were breweries centuries old producing smoked beers as their fathers had done before them. This part of the trip made me feel so small, yet proud to be a part of this industry. What surprised me during this stage of our investigations was the empathy and balance our task required. Ray and I both have a profound respect for the history contained in this industry, but respect is not as easy emotionally to balance with the reporting job. The toughest thing for me was coming to terms with breweries that were hundreds of years old but that made me shudder at their lack of attention to the maintenance of their brewing equipment, and their disregard to sound brewing techniques as I understood them. If a brewery had been around for 300 years, who am I to criticize it? Other old breweries had recently retooled and were gems that had balanced their historical roots with the need to keep the plant running for another hundred years. Balancing historical practice with that of modern techniques and cleanliness was done by many beautiful small breweries. I may sound naive, but it was a bit of a revelation to realize that all breweries need to renew themselves and that if a brewery is over 300 years old, it has reinvented itself numerous times. The fact that all breweries are somewhere on this cycle allowed me to understand the continuum of which we are all a part. The young breweries that had just started up in places like Japan, the United States, and all over the globe that are barely ten years old are a part of this cycle along with those that are hundreds of years old. The need that all breweries share is the need to reinvent themselves, melding the new with the old. Breweries can only survive if they are maintained, and renewal is necessary. The trick is balancing what is historically significant with the need to produce as good a beer as is possible.

In the past, I have done research at the Library of Congress, which supposedly has the most complete collection of published work in the United States. However, when I called them concerning the subject of smoke flavor in beer, they said I needed to find the private Hurty Peck Collection. After a long search, I found that the library at University of California–Davis had just recently purchased this collection. When I got there and started to read the old texts, I fell into a cloud of research euphoria. The awe that I felt while reading manuscripts written in the sixteenth century touched me in the most profound way. While looking for any and all references to fire, smoke, and malt kilning, I ran across one reference that listed the four elements of brewing as earth, wind, water, and fire. Aristotle had stated that these elements were what all matter was made of in circa 350 B.C., and here I was reading texts that viewed brewing chemistry in these terms! It was during these moments where it was difficult to concentrate on the pure subject of smoke. The librarians at UC–Davis were remarkably helpful, and in discussions with them they mentioned issues that I had to reconcile. Books were written for men by men, yet women who did the brewing at home typically could not read. Therefore while our literary research focused more on the industrial state of the art, what was brewed at home or in the small villages could only be guessed at—although we are sure it was appreciated for its sustenance and thoroughly enjoyed.

During the library research I thought a lot about how and why smoke is perceived as it is and how it was perceived historically. When open fires were the primary heat, cooking, and lighting source, smoke aroma must have been everywhere in the community, just as it is around a campfire. Therefore, why then would it be mentioned if it was the norm? I feel tempted to surmise that smoke aroma was only referred to when it was not there, or when it was extraordinarily intense. Our ancestors who depended upon the warmth and security of fire may have had some appreciation for its flavor, but why would they mention it if it was always there? The most difficult part of this project was that we had to summarize and focus our investigations; we couldn't just follow them wherever they and our active imaginations took us.

At Alaskan Brewing Company, we have been brewing smoked beers since 1988. Each year, a week of my life seems to be grounded in the mechanics of malt smoking for that particular year's batch of Alaskan Smoked Porter. Sandro Lane of Taku Smokeries has helped with every batch of smoked malt we have used in the production of our smoked porter, and I have met with him every year to discuss the smoking schedule. Sandro's business is fish processing and smoking. One reason we meet is that we have always had to work around the commercial fishing schedule where delivery of the massive fish catches sometimes require the smokehouse to be cleaned and put on standby while all hands are on deck. These times are when we can use Sandro's smokehouse for malt. We use specially made malt screens that have been darkened by use in the smokehouse over the years. They stay in a corner of the brewery, and every time I walk by the area it reminds me of the first time Sandro and I used them to smoke the first test batch of malt. That first batch followed a hot-smoke program and imparted too intense a flavor that overpowered the porter we were using as a base beer. With subsequent batches using more of a cold-smoke approach, we finally hit the balance of characteristics we wanted. Is the fact that the shortest nerves to the brain are those of the olfactory system indicative of their importance? We clearly react to smells even though we don't talk about it much. As we unload the smoking screens in preparation for making this year's batch of smoked malt, the alderwood smoke aroma left from many previous seasons permeates the area and brings smiles to us all. The good life is here.

The smokehouse is now cleaned, and it is not going to be used for smoking fish for ten days. We will roast malt for the next seven days, around the clock, in order to make enough malt for one batch of Smoked Porter. As in all of the smokehouses and some of the malt houses in Alaska a hundred years ago, we will use alder as fuel to roast the malt. For the next week, all I will think about is the smell of smoke. I will taste each batch of grain fresh from the smokehouse as we get the next batch ready. The smoke is overwhelming, and (as is typical) after a while you wonder if the malt is as smoky as you remembered it. I know it must be, but that is one of the repeated questions that I ask myself every year. The first day I am painstakingly careful about the cleanliness of the smokehouse, as just the smallest bit of fish oil will ruin the head retention of the entire batch of beer. By the second day my pallet has become saturated with smoke, and I can hardly tell if the malt is smoked enough. I worry about the moisture and the humidity as all of these factors will affect how the smoke will condense upon the malt as the malt is heated. After seven days of smoking, we then will transport all the smoked malt to the brewery where the malt will be stored in the cooler until it is time to mash. When it is time to brew the Smoked Porter, we have one shot at it, as the window for smoking is past. As the crushed malt is dropped into the mash tun, the smell of roasted smoked malt wafts through the brewery. Is it as smoky as last year? Everyone thinks so, but smoke is such an emotional aroma it is so hard for me to be sure.

Ray and I are writing about a flavor component that existed in beer's history, yet historically wasn't always referred to favorably. This circumstance could have been because smoke was quite common and was not an easily controlled component in the heating processes of years gone by. Thus it wasn't always a desired by-product. Today, smoke is controlled, and it can be a beautiful flavor complement to beer. I had such a positive experience while writing this book, exploring old traditions and new ideas that impart smoke flavor to beer. I hope I have added something of value to the understanding of smoke-flavored beers—I had fun trying!

—Geoffrey Larson

CHAPTER 1

History of Smoke in Beer

Other books in the Classic Beer Style Series have included history sections that carefully traced the origins and development of distinct, individual beer styles. In the cases of porter, India pale ale, Pilsener, and even bock, there are very clear delineations of the style over time. Since the establishment of these and other styles there has rarely been a question about what their names stood for with regard to beer.

Then we come to the more difficult cases. In his last work in the Classic Beer Style Series, one of us—Ray—tackled the history of brown ales. Tracking the history of what we think of today as a style called brown ale proved somewhat tricky. The word *brown* is a convenient descriptor for beer. As a result, a good many beers have been described in the beer literature as "brown ales" or "brown beers" simply to distinguish them from pale or even wheat-based brews.

And so it is with smoked beer. It is clear that many, if not most beers—regardless of other features—were smoky at one time. But unlike the case of brown ale—which resolved into a fairly well defined modern style, the haphazard appearance of smoke across a range of different beers has not changed. Indeed, anyone who has ever sat at a judging table and been presented with a flight of twelve smoked beers knows that this is less a beer style than a flavor characteristic that can be applied to nearly any beer. Furthermore, smoke is not a one-dimensional flavor. Just as there is no one aroma of "smoke," so too is there no single "smoke" flavor. When you say *smoke,* is that beechwood smoke or peat smoke? Are you imagining the smell of burning alderwood or the character of burning mesquite? Would you fuel your fire with corncobs or cherry tree trimmings?

So although the range of smoked beers available in any one community today may seem rather narrow, the subject of smoked beer in general is tremendously broad. And if we look back 300 or 400 years—back to the beginnings of commercial beer production and the real emergence of beer styles as we know them today—then we have defined a subject matter that is not only broad, but also quite deep.

Both of us love the history of brewing and beer. If given the chance, we would have spent many weeks pondering the details of ancient texts that mention *smoke* or the German translation *rauch* in some context or another, pondered the construction of malt kilns both ancient and modern, and ferreted through every recipe available in search of new brews that may have been touched by smoke. We've stopped short of that—although given the length of this chapter, you may wonder what we left out!

Here's what we have in mind. First, we want to wax somewhat rhapsodic over smoke itself. We like smoked beers (and smoked meats and smoked cheeses and, yes, even smoked teas), so we want to try to infect you with a bit of that enthusiasm before we settle down to the job of sorting fact from fiction when it comes to the history of smoked beer. So without further ado, here's some of the fun and fancy of brewing smoked beer.

The Flame and Firkin, or, "Look What They've Done to My Beer, Ma"

Before the rise of commercial brewing, the production of beer was a domestic art, practiced in households far and wide. The well-off had servants to brew for them, although the common household made beer for its own consumption. Queen Elizabeth I drank beer for breakfast, made by the royal brewers. Meanwhile in Norwegian houses, it was not unusual that the commoners had malt bins hung under the beams of the living-room ceiling and wooden boxes that could be lowered over the hearth. Boasts were made claiming that a particularly good flavor was given to the ale made at home because of the home-smoked malt (Nordland, 1969, p. 19). As commerce progressed, beer was also made for sale by specialists. The ale wives sold ale for personal profit. The inns needed to feed the common folk staying at their establishment, and the monasteries needed to supply this necessity to their monks and the traveling nobility.

Malting in the Celtic nations around A.D. 410 is described by Isidorus and Orosius (White, 1860, p. 12). By some accounts, it may have been Julius Caesar in 55 B.C. that brought the malting technique to Britain

(White, 1860, p. 12). Others say beer brewing came via a more northerly route from Babylon (Corran, 1975, p. 24).

Among the many types of beer made in Sumeria in circa 2800 B.C., there is an interesting reference to a type of black beer called *kas-gig* (Lutz, 1922, p. 86). This beer is mentioned as being the cheapest common beer of the time. The brewer of the black beer was called the "man of the beer loaf." Loaves were made of ground, germinated grain, which was then baked. On the east wall of the tomb of Rahenem, it is shown pictorially that dough in open vessels was stacked for baking in a manner that directly exposed the tops of the loaves to a slow fire. Perhaps smoke character was introduced at this stage, and likely the color of the beer in this region depended upon the charring of the loaves of dough. To actually make the beer, the loaves were broken up and soaked in water with leavening, allowed to sit for a few days, and then filtered through woven baskets and possibly bottled in pitch-lined earthenware. The malting as described during the early written history of Egyptian brewing seems to have taken advantage of air drying, which makes sense (Lutz, 1922, pp. 79–80).

Archeological finds in southwest Norway show that around A.D. 500–600, malt was dried on a flat stone on top of a hearth or on the top stone of a flueless corner stove (Nordland, 1969, p. 28). This use of a heated surface continued into more modern times in Norway, as was reported by a writer named Jensson in 1646. Jensson talked of the sporadic use of a technique called *turkebrye* employing hot stones in a wooden trough that would be stirred with the malt to dry the grains (Nordland, 1969, p. 26). Was this an attempt to lessen the smoke character by indirect heating? Even references about brewing in Einbeck, c. 1203, imply that some brewers avoided kiln-dried malt in order to keep the beer clearer (Anonymous, 1903, p. 20). Malting was a very central part of the household in the northern climates. In Norway, the main part of the house was used to malt grains for brewing, and in southern Norway, the bath house was also used for malting and drying. Often there was a separate building for malting called a *kjolne*, which was constructed with two floors. This type of building is very similar to the Swedish houses of the same function (Nordland, 1969, p. 24). Probably the reason for separate buildings had more to do with fire hazards than specialization of the process. In the Baltic countries and Russia, the malting building was called a *ria*. In this structure the ground floor has an open fire or a special but primitive stove from which both heat and smoke rise up to the second floor. The transition between the floors was usually a grate of sorts that held the malt but allowed heated air to pass through. This grate was often made of wood and was overlaid with horse and cattle hair. Mats of hair for malt-drying applications are mentioned throughout beer-making references pertaining to Scandinavia,Germany, the Netherlands, and England. Sometimes holes were drilled in the wooden interface, and the matted grains were kept from falling through because the rootlets acted to bind the grain together. The fact that the second floor was usually larger than the first allowed a walking area not heated directly underneath. There was a hole in one of the gables to allow the smoke to escape.

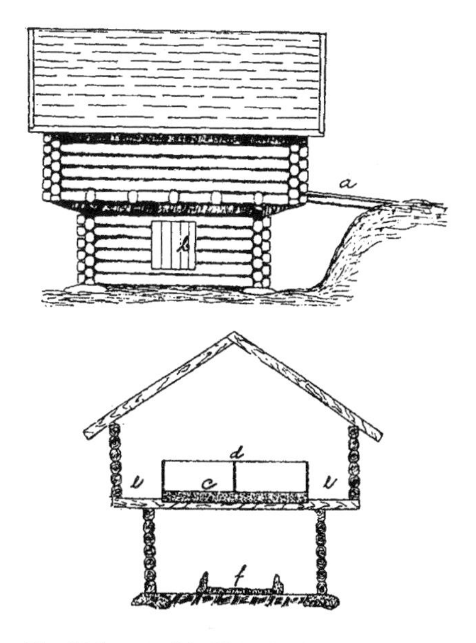

The kjolne used in Norway was a specialized smoke kiln for making malt. (a) access to the balcony, (b) the hearth, (c) the porous support for the green malt usually of horse hair over a floor with holes, (d) the malt bins to contain the malt on top of the heated floor, (e) the cool floor cantilevered away from the hearth and (f) the open fire pit which generated heat that rose to the balcony to dry the grain.

There were other, smaller kilns called *kylne* or *sonn* that operated by similar principles, but they were of one-room construction; the smoke and heat were forced into contact with the malt. There is linguistic evidence that the Vikings got the *kjolne* from the Anglo-Saxons and the *sonn* from the Irish. Such kilns continued to be used, even after the local mills had taken over the drying of the grain, as only this method produced the "right traditional flavor." Those farms that no longer had kilns of this sort would take their malt to farms that did (Nordland, 1969, p. 28–29). As the local mills were specialists in drying grain, they were more efficient with their fuel, which probably minimized any smoke character in the malt. There is no question that malt made in these types of kilns had a smoky character, and in fact smoke flavor was desired.

Malting was supervised very closely for reasons of taxation but also to ensure its brewing quality. In a quote from circa 1500, numerous shortcomings of malt are identified, but smoke is not mentioned among them.

> clene swete and drye and wele made, not capped in sakkes [this trick of putting good stuff on the top and something inferior below must not be tried] nor raw-dried, dank, or wete malte or made of mowe

> brent [burnt or over-heated in the mow or stack] belyed [swollen] malte, edgrove [germinating] malte acrespired [sprouting at both ends] wyvell eaten or medled malte. (Strong, 1954, p. 16)

But by the mid-1700s, we see a clear issue with smoke, either the type or the intensity, as being an undesirable.

> Coak is reckonded by most to exceed all others for making drink of the finest Flavor and pale Color, because it sends no smoak forth to hurt the Malt with any offensive tang,... Straw is the next sweetest Fuel, but Wood and Fern worst of all. (Ellis, 1737, p. 8)

Beer was made in as many ways as there were local traditions and with whatever raw materials were at hand. In the following quotation there is a description from Sir More about his travels and experiences with the quality of the malts he encountered across the English countryside.

> In the Southern Countries ... they take more time than in other parts, and dry in liesurely with Pit-Coal Charkt, called in some Places Coak, and in others, Culm, which is sweet and gives a gentle and

> certain heat. Whereas in the South East parts, they dry their Malt with Straw, which is hard to keep to a moderate and equal heat. And in the West Countrys with Wood, which gives a most ingrateful Tack to such as are not by Custom familiarized to it. (More, 1703, p. 58–59)

The methods of production would have been as varied as the people that employed them. We need to think back to a time when not only every city had a different beer, but every home had a different beer. Women made the beer in the home, and at that time women were not taught to read. Women taught their daughters how to brew beer, and that oral tradition carried forward many diverse and traditional methods. Books written on the subject may have been for the head of household to teach his staff in the way he wanted his

An illustration from "Dictionarium Domesticum" a household dictionary in 1736 depicting the woman of the household amidst her brewing duties.

beer brewed (King, 1947, p. 110), but the books may not have been used by the women doing the brewing.

Although literature shows that smoke was an important flavor in beer (good or bad), the diversity of this flavor in beer and ale is unimaginable. Fuels are the direct source of smoke, and many things dictated what was used as fuel. Cost, availability, and the impact on the quality of the malt are obvious issues that influenced which fuel was selected, but there were others. One reference to straw as an important fuel source for brewing had more to do with the dangers of fires being started by the use of this much less controllable (i.e., more volatile) fuel. This regulation came in the form of a decree framed by the City Council of London in 1189 and reproduced here from King (1947, p. 22) in more modern language:

> All ale-houses be forbidden except those which shall be licensed by the common council of the city Guild-hall, excepting those belonging to persons who will build of stone, that the city may secure. And that no baker or ale wife brew, by night, either with reeds or straw or stubble, but with wood only.

So although this reference concerns the prevention of fires in London, it shows that ale-houses and ale wives, which brewed the beer they served, were directed to brew with wood instead of straw. One can clearly see that government regulations could and did impact the presence of wood smoke in ale and beer. Straw was often used preferentially over other fuels, but in this case, government edict restricted its use.

In 1307, London brewers, dyers, and lime burners were forbidden to burn coal because the air pollution was so bad in London. The widespread use of sea coal, a low-grade coal, had a poor reputation anyway because of

> the prevailing opinion that the smell and dirt of sea-coal fire would be transmitted to the taste of the ale. This prejudice prevented any wholesale adoption of coal … in brewing in England before Elizabethan times. (Corran, 1975, p. 78–79)

The making of malt and the drying of it via directly heated air are thoroughly documented. The references to smoke in beer start out as merely the recognition of the type of fuel and its effects on the manufacturing of malt and the subsequent effect on the flavor of beer.

In *Description of England* (1577, chapter VI, Book II, as mentioned by Corran, 1975, p. 60), the author William Harrison dealt with the food and diet of the English and gave specific details as to domestic malting and brewing. He indicated that wood and straw were used for drying the malt, but that straw was preferred.

Wood was becoming scarce in England in the mid-sixteenth century. In 1543, an Act of Parliament stipulated that every exporter must import as much clapboard as would be taken out of the country in the form of wooden casks. The destruction of forests following the development of commerce gave cause for alarm (Corran, 1975, pp. 65–66) and also limited wood as a fuel source.

In 1610, William Slingsby and his partners petitioned for a patent to use coal to replace all boiling processes, but specifically excluded kilning of malt where the acceptable wood smoke would be superior to coal (Corran, 1975, p. 79).

Later in the 1600s, Welch coal or culm became the preferred fuel. The terms *Welch coal* and *culm* refer to a type of anthracite. Anthracite is a much purer form of carbon than other coals. It is low in sulfur and produces a much more easily controlled, virtually smokeless heat.

Although the manufacture of coke had begun earlier in the 1700s, the first reported use of coke by a brewer was in 1723. Coke is made by the partial combustion of coal in a process much like making charcoal out of wood. This process takes a low grade of coal and, by heating it, drives off many waxes, tars, sulfurous compounds, and volatile organic chemicals.

In 1729, a Professor Bradley wrote "The Riches of a Hop Garden Explained" (Corran, 1975, p. 96), and in it he accounts,

> The malt from the Northern counties was excellent, owing to the use of coke in the drying kilns. In the south-east straw was used and in the West Country wood, the former being difficult to control [and] the latter imparting a most ungrateful taste.

But these new fuels were hard to come by, were expensive, and became cost prohibitive if any distance for shipping was involved. Distances of 30 miles from a shipping center, like London, were cost prohibitive. Also if even the smallest coal chunks got into the coke, it would ruin any advantage the coke gave to the malt flavor (Stopes, 1885, pp. 28–32).

On July 20, 1635, Nicholase Halse took a patent for the first indirectly heated malt kiln (Patent No. 85) (King, 1947, p. 90) "making a Kyll for drying malt and hops with sea-cole, turf, or anie fewel, without touching smoke" (Stopes, 1885, p. 10).

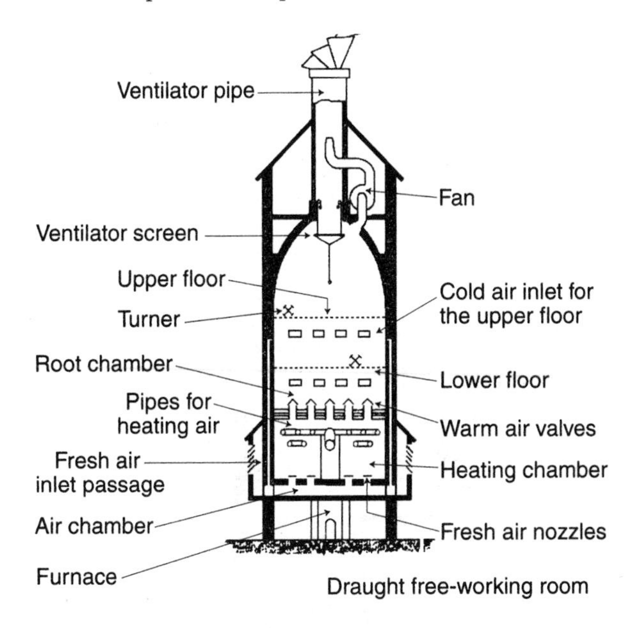

A smoke-less malt kilm which used indirectly heated air to dry the malt.

Twelve months later, Sir Nicholase Halse had a very similar patent, and two years later in 1637, Thomas, Earl of Berks, patented another kiln for drying malt, hops, etc.

(Stopes, 1885, p. 10). This type of kiln allowed all manner of fuels to be used, a choice that could have had a profound effect on the economics of malting. Any fuel used would impart no flavor to the malt. Brewing technology was constantly advancing; however, not all were quick to embrace change. In Scotland, malt was still being made by using a technique of drying with wood at the final stages (Roberts, 1846, p. 204). Even in England, texts

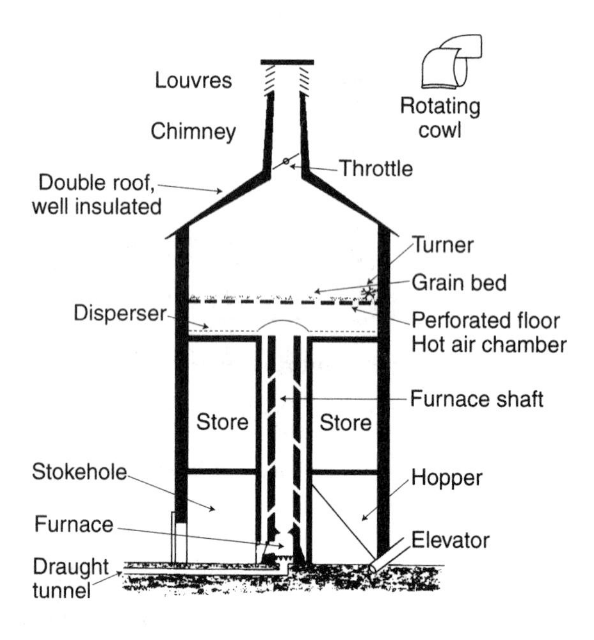

A tradition direct-fired kiln often referred to as a smoke kiln.

were still endorsing techniques that used wood in direct-fired kilns to dry moist malt as late as 1878 (Steel, 1878, p. 22). In places like the fledgling United States, it appears that much of the equipment being used was of the direct drier type (Wahl and Henius, 1901, p. 601). Such equipment would make it likely that a discernible smoked character could have been associated with the malt. Although indirect-fire kilns did not come into common use in many countries until the twentieth century, as we will see, other changes drove the smoke from malt.

Putting Some Stakes in the Ground

The problem with history is that the modern world won't stand still while you study the past. Every time you think you know exactly what happened back there, some new bit of knowledge comes to light—some new text presents opportunities for interpretation. We have given you a flavor for the interesting aspects of the history of smoked beer in the preceding section. Now, for the remainder of this chapter on history, we'll focus our presentation on two key questions.

The first of these questions is simple: When did smoke cease to be a regular and accepted characteristic of beer flavor? Here we attempt to trace the presence of smoke in beer through the brewing literature of both Britain and Germany. In so doing, we explore the attitudes that brewers and drinkers have had toward smoke at various times over the past few centuries.

The second question more directly addresses the characteristics of beers that included smoked flavor: What types of deliberately smoked beers have been brewed since smoke stopped being ubiquitous in beer? As a corollary to this question, we'll ask, What do we know about the character of these beers in general and as well as with regard to their smoke character?

With this game plan established, we should make one further note. This part of the discussion is limited almost entirely to the German and British brewing scenes, with an occasional reference to latter-day North American practice. The reasons for this approach are simple. Britain was the great brewing nation of the eighteenth and early nineteenth centuries; Germany assumed this role around the middle of the nineteenth century and held it for most—if not all—of the twentieth century. Thus, most of the historical literature about brewing during the period of our interest comes from one of these two countries. Although we recognize that beer was brewed in other cultures and that other smoked beers must surely have existed, we unfortunately have not been able to access documentation.

Despite this shortcoming, we believe that you will find the history of smoke—and of smoke-flavored beers—to be interesting and informative. Furthermore, parts of the history lay the groundwork for recipes presented later in the book and thus make the information not only informative, but relevant to the appreciation of beers you may soon be brewing.

Ubiquitous Smoke

Most brewers writing about the history of beer build a wall at the beginning of the eighteenth century. The "invention" of pale malt occurred at about this time (c. 1680–1700), they say, tied to the introduction of coke as a smokeless, controllable fuel source. Prior to that, many believe, all beers were smoky and brown because all malts were dried over a wood fire. Although this statement is not entirely true, as we will see, it appears to have been largely the case.

Prior to the devastating romp of The Plague though Europe in 1348–1349, the production of ale or beer was an entirely domestic activity. This circumstance, combined with the paucity of surviving documents from the period, makes it impossible for us to extend our examination of beer character to these early years.

However, in the time between the Black Death and the creation of porter in 1720, the nature of brewing in Britain changed considerably. Hops were introduced, which increased the storage possibilities of beer and thus allowed it to be transported and inventoried for the purposes of commerce. As a result of this development—as well as increasing trade and urbanization—brewing shifted from a strictly domestic art to that of a trade in which specialization and volume production led to the development of brewing as an early industry.

The most important issues in our efforts to understand this period relate to the character and use of the key ingredient, malt. Malt is the soul of beer, they say. And there can be no question that it lies at the heart of the smoked-beer issue. For if the malt was smoky, then the ales made from it were likely to be smoky as well.

Before 1700, in texts of the time and in the recipes that survive, the ingredient "malt" is often listed with no further distinction or description. For instance, a recipe dating to the early 1500s calls for "10 quarters of malt, 2 quarters of wheat and 2 of oats" (Corran, 1975, pp. 50–51; Anonymous, 1903, p. 32). And, although coal and coke were to become the favored fuels of the industrial age, we know that the earlier malts were dried in a different way.

One option was air drying. During this period, it appears that some malt was air-dried outdoors during warm weather and even, at times, indoors. These malts might be produced by the brewer and thus were used in a very short time. As a result, they did not need to be dried to the same level that we expect today in order to be stored, transported, and kept at the brewery before use. Although we can't say just exactly how prevalent air-dried malt may have been, one thing is certain: the malt produced this way would have been very pale and, of course, smoke free. Other techniques for drying that were smoke free or nearly so were probably also used, such as spreading the malt on a large flat stone above the oven and so forth.

Although kilnless, smokeless drying was an alternative, it is clear that small kilns were widely available. Thus, much of the malt during this time was probably dried on a kiln of one sort or another. Various sources discuss the use of wood, straw, and fern as fuel for such kilns. Each brought different features to the kilning and to the finished malt itself—which we further discuss subsequently.

As for the smokiness that might have been imparted to these malts, we find frequent evidence that it was unwanted, if not entirely avoided. A description published in 1542 by one Andrew Boorde (Anonymous, 1903, p. 32) described the desirable properties of ale: "it must be freshe and cleare, it must not be ropy nor smoky."

Corran (1975, p. 96) noted that, during the sixteenth century, "wood or straw was used for drying, the latter being preferred." Related to this, Harrison (1577 [1994], p. 136) said, "the straw-dried is the most excellent. For the wood-dried malt, when it is brewed, beside that the drink is higher [darker] of color, it doth hurt and annoy the head of him that is not used thereto, because of the smoke." From these descriptions, we feel confident that some smokeless malts were indeed available even before coal and coke came along.

Another factor would be that of kiln design. Beginning in the early 1600s we find reference to kilns that prevent contact between smoke and malt. The treatise by Markham in 1615 (as quoted by Cindy Renfrow, 1998) describes a "French kiln" that burns "any kind of fuel whatsoever, and neither shall the smoke offend or breed ill taste in the malt, nor yet discolor it, as many times it doth in open kilns." This description is followed by one for the "West Country kiln made at the end of a kitchen range or chimney, which dries the malt by hot air, with no smoke."

Finally, Corran (1975, p. 80) reviewed brewing-related patents given out during the seventeenth century. The first patent in any subject connected with brewing appeared in 1634, and altogether fourteen appeared before the end of the century. The interesting point is that thirteen out of the fourteen deal with fuel and heating problems. We may draw the following conclusions from them: (1) that smoke was a great nuisance in the drying of malt; (2) that the ale and beer brewed from smoked malt was "unsavoury and unwholesome," but presumably must have been widely known and accepted to a considerable extent, and (3) that straw, wood, peat, and turf were already being supplanted by coal, both in the drying of malt and hops and in the boiling of coppers.

These observations tell us that smoky-flavored brown-colored ales were probably common in pre-industrial Britain. They also tell us that even at this early time, many brewers—and presumably consumers as well—disliked smoke and sought to remove it from their malts and beers. Although smoky brown beers most likely dominated the scene, others more pale and smoke free were certainly known as well.

Within the spectrum of "smoky" beers, one probably found a broad range of smoke expressions: some that were tarry or creosote-like, some that delivered a piercing phenolic note, and still others that included a pleasant earthy wood note. Exactly which flavors were present and how they were perceived, we will never know. Still it is worth remembering that smoke can be either pleasant or foul and that the complaints lodged about smoke may have indicated cases where the flavor—always present in some form—had merely ventured over into an unpleasant expression as we know is possible.

Dawning of the Industrial Age

As the eighteenth century opened (and surviving brewing literature begans to become available to modern researchers), we found that brewers and maltsters have become divided into separate businesses to a significant degree. The *London and Country Brewer*, the best-known source of brewing literature from the eighteenth century, regularly discussed the practices of maltsters and

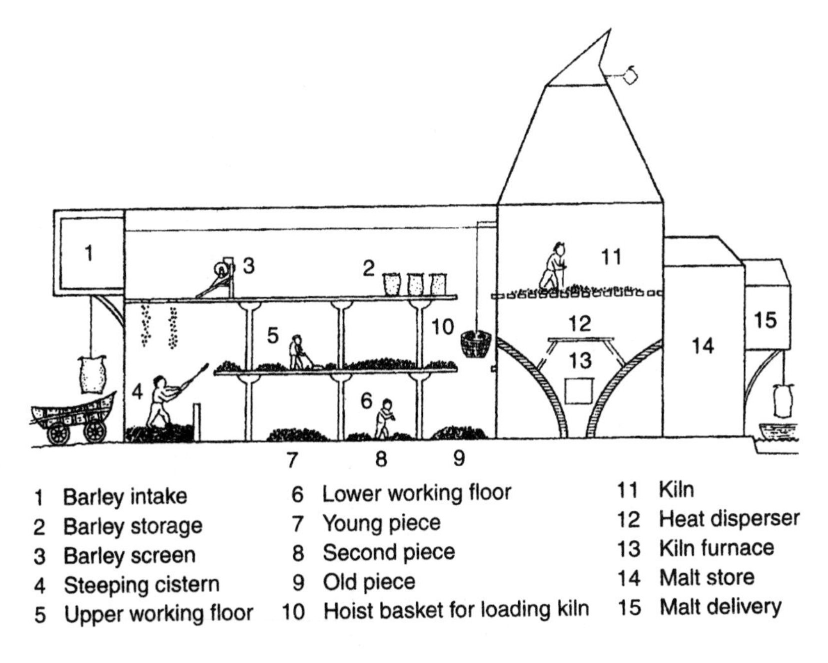

A commercial malt house depicted in the early 1800s as a specialized business.

brewers as separate crafts, noting in many places the interactions between the two. Indeed, most subsequent English brewing texts have devoted themselves to one discipline or the other.

It is easy to see why malting would evolve as an independent business. At any significant scale, it requires specialized equipment—notably a kiln—little suited to other uses and costly to acquire. In addition, both the raw material and the finished product can be kept for many months without spoiling—making them suitable for transportation and storage by either the maker or the user. In addition, for any one maltster there must have been many possible suppliers of barley as well as numerous potential customers for the malt. So, here in a neat package, we find all the elements necessary for commerce.

Early malting operations may have been akin to some of today's farmers' cooperatives: a farmer would grow his own barley and make his own beer, but he used the services of a maltster to accomplish the critical transformation that came in between. Domestic brewers who evolved into commercial breweries might well have continued to patronize independent maltsters both because of a lack of knowledge about the craft of malting and a lack of capital for acquiring the needed land and equipment. At the same time, of course, some maltsters were also brewers, and in numerous places, the two crafts coexisted under a single roof.

We mention the division between malting and brewing because of its impact on the smokiness in malt. For even though many lamented the presence of smoke in beer, it continued to exist for a considerable time. Maltsters, driven by the need for profits, had to make malt cheaply in order to compete for business. Direct-fired kilns and natural-fiber fuels (wood, straw, ferns, etc.) were the cheapest way to produce a saleable product, even though it then carried some of the flavor of these fuels.

The *London and Country Brewer* (Ellis, 1742, p. 320) spent some considerable time lamenting the errors and evils that maltsters indulged in to ensure their survival or boost their success. It seems that the production of "quality" malt was not an easy sale, as indicated by this passage:

> [A] Quaker Maltster of this Town was so careful in making a true, healthful, pleasant pale Malt that he was six and thirty Hours drying one Kiln of it with Welch Coal; but his careful Honesty brought him under a Loss, for he afterwards broke, by being obliged to sell this delicate Malt at the same Price of others, that were dried in eight or twelve Hours Time at a much cheaper Rate.

This situation was further compounded by the fact that some brewers managed to produce beer that was fairly smoke-free even when wood was used to dry a portion of the malt (Ellis, 1742, p. 255):

> Wood Fuel is made use of in some Kilns, which though it yields a bad Smoke, that gives an unpleasant Tang to the Malt, and its Drink, yet, by Skill in the Management of it, its unpleasant Quality may be much lessen'd. At Beasonsfield I have tasted a tolerable good common Ale, brewed with a Mixture of six Bushels of pale Malt, dried with Coak, and seven Bushels of brown, dried with Beech Wood.

Perhaps this was one maltster-brewer who had found the key to delivering the pleasant characteristics of smoke without the less desirable flavors that can come from it.

Finally, two other factors probably contributed to the acceptance of smoky brown malt during the early 1700s.

First, coal and coke were taxed, making their use for the production of any kind of malt rather expensive. Pale malt produced from these fuels *was* available and was used in making pale ales throughout the eighteenth century, but the resulting product was too expensive for mass consumption.

Second, the hydrometer, that most basic tool of brewing, had not yet been invented. Indeed, the first treatise on its use in brewing was not published until 1785, and widespread acceptance did not come for another decade or so. Without a hydrometer, brewers could not detect the false economy of brown malt over its pale competitor. Nearly every brewer today knows that pale malt gives you more extract per pound than chocolate malt. But without a hydrometer, brewers of the 1700s could not see that brown malt—which was cheaper by the pound—was more costly than pale malt when considered in terms of extract yield.

The combination of all these influences can be seen in comments such as the following (Ellis, 1742, p. 178):

> Which leads me to take Notice of what, in my humble Opinion, is a Mismanagement in some Brewers, who for Cheapness sake will buy Wood-dried brown Malt, commonly made on Kilns without a Hair-cloth, for brewing the common Butt-Brown-beers, sometimes at sixteen Shillings per Quarter, when the Pale Sort is at two and twenty Shillings, or four and twenty Shillings. As believing the smoky Tang, by Time and the great Quantity of Hops, will be over come. But I have known many Instances, where the Hop has overcome such Drink by the Smallness of its Body. And no Wonder such blood-red Beer has more Colour than Strength, since the Brewer, by the

> low Price he will have the Malt at forces the Maltster to make it accordingly.

Thus it is that conditions conspired to sustain the use of smoky brown malts in Britain long after their flavor had been decried by the purists of the brewing community. Having established this fact, let us look more closely at the fuels that were used and the malts that were made with them.

Fueling the Fire

During the eighteenth century, it seems that nearly every possible fuel was used to stoke the fires that dried malt. We see repeated references to those most desired: coke, Welch coal, and related materials. But we see even more frequent reference to the fibrous fuels such as wood, straw, and the like. Finally, we see some oddball elements such as sea coal and even cow dung playing a role in this regard.

Although this was a time of transition and conflict—with newcomers coal and coke competing with the standard woods and straws—it was also a time when brewing science was coming into full bloom. Thus we have considerable documentation of the character of these different fuels and their application to the art of malting from the texts of the day. Since no other source we have seen addresses this subject so thoroughly at any point in history, we feel it is useful and informative to review these observations here. All of the observations given in this section come from the fourth edition of the *London and Country Brewer*, published in 1742 and written by William Ellis.

First, let us comment that even though kilns were readily available through maltsters of various types, some use of air drying still persisted, as our chronicler reports (p. 254), "He also was a nice Person, that had his Malt dried on Leads, thro Glass Windows, by the Sun only."

In addition, hops as well as some malts were already being dried in kilns that delivered an indirect heat (p. 253):

> Contrary to this too quick Way is the slow Cockle-Oast Kiln, which dries Hops or Malt with hot Air, the sweetest of any Way; and that by Means of the four cast Irons, I wrote of in my last Book, in which they burn common Sea-Coal, whose foul, offensive Smoke is conveyed away by a Chimney.

Clearly, however, most malts produced during this age were dried on direct-fired kilns. These kilns varied primarily in the structure of the platform that supported the malt during drying. The most highly regarded were the hair-cloth kilns, next the wire-screen kilns, and finally the iron plate or tile platforms. All afforded direct access to the malt for the heat and smoke from the fire.

Now we move on to the subject of fuels for kilns. Let us first address the issue of coke and coal, which seem to have been used primarily for the production of pale malt. On this subject, we find no shortage of commentary, of which two examples follow:

> Coak is recokoned by most to exceed all others for making Drink of the finest Flavour and pale Colour, because it sends no Smoak forth to hurt the Malt with any offensive Tang, that Wood, Fern, and Straw are apt to do in a lesser or greater Degree. . . . (p. 8)

> Pale and Amber Malts dried with Coak or Culm, obtain a more clean, bright, pale Colour, than if dried with any other Fuel, because there is not Smoak to darken and sully their Skins or Husks, and give them an ill Relish, that those Malts little or more have, which are dried with Straw, Wood, or Fern, etc. The Coak or Welch Coal also makes more true and compleat Malt, as I have before hinted, than any other Fuel because its Fire gives both a

> gentle and certain Heat, whereby the Corns are in all their Parts gradually dried and therefore of late these Malts have gained such a Reputation that the great Quantities have been consumed in most Parts of the Nation for their wholesome Natures and sweet fine Taste. (p. 13)

Despite these generally glowing reviews for coal, its early use was not without some interesting, if perhaps short-lived, innovations (p. 254): "So in Nottinghamshire they sift their smallest Pit Coal, and work it up with Cow Dung, in the Form of Bricks, in the Summer Time, and in Winter they dry their Malt with them." One cannot help but wonder what the beer made from this malt would have tasted like!

After coke and coal, straw seemed to be the most highly regarded fuel (p. 8): "Straw is the next sweetest Fuel." Our author waxes eloquent on the superior properties of wheat straw:

> This Fuel, tho' it is one of the most ancient Sorts, still keeps its Reputation, so that when it is in due Order, and managed by a skilful Hand, none exceeds it for drying of both pale and brown Malt, for Brewing either Ales or Strong-beers: Because,

> I suppose Wheat-straw to be in a thorough dry Condition when it is used. . . . From hence it is that the Smoke of this sweet Fuel is so little prejudicial to the Malt, and I must own, that, in all my Travels, I never tasted any Malt-Liquor more pleasant than that dryed with Wheat-straw. . . . But this delicate fuel is refused by many for two Reasons; First, because it is somewhat dearer than some other Sorts; Secondly, because it requires the Care of two Men to a Kiln; for here the Fireman is obliged to give such close Attendance that he cannot leave his Place to turn the Malt; whereas, with Wood, Coak, or Coal Fuels, the Fireman can do both. (p. 178)

For those situations in which wheat straw was not available, our advisor offers comment on some other options (p. 255): "Wheat Straw under a Hair-Cloth is reckoned the best Fuel by most, Rye-Straw next and Wheat Haulm worse." We note here that whereas straw consists of "stems and stalks, especially dry and separated by threshing," haulm was straw "as left after gathering the ears" and obviously subjected to weathering or some other treatment that lessened its value as fuel.

Despite his praises for straw generally, our author admits to its weaknesses in a different passage (p. 13): "but as the Fire of the Straw is not so regular as the Coak, the Malt is attended with more Uncertainty in its Making, because it is difficult to keep it to a moderate and equal Heat, and also exposes the Malt in some Degree to the Taste of the Smoak."

The bottom line on all straw came down to this: it was better than wood but not as good as coke or coal. Of course, the use of coke or coal was reserved for the production of pale malts; thus our author concludes that straw is the most desirable fuel for the making of brown malt (p. 13): "Brown Malts are dried with Straw, Wood, and Fern, etc. The Straw-dried is far the best." And further (p. 254): "The best Pale Malt is dried with Coak, Charcoal, or Welch Coal, or with Coak and Welch Coal together, and the best Brown with Wheat Straw."

Despite the clear preference that *London and Country Brewer* author William Ellis expressed for the use of coke or straw in the making of malt, it seems clear from his descriptions that most brown malt was dried over a wood fire. And since the most popular beer of the age, porter, was made from such malt, it was no doubt in great demand. Thus a good deal of Ellis's text discusses the properties of various woods and their use. Here is his opening shot (p. 13):

> Brown Malts are dried with Straw, Wood, and Fern, etc. the Straw-dried is far the best, but the Wood-sort has a most unnatural Taste, that few can bear with, but the Necessitous, and those that are accustomed to its strong smoaky Tang; yet it is much used in some of the Western Parts of England, and many thousand Quarterns of this Malt have been formerly used in London for brewing the Butt-Keeping Beers with, and that because it sold for two Shillings per Quartern, cheaper than the Straw-dried Malt; nor was this Quality of the Wood-dried Malt much regarded by some of its Brewers, for that its ill Taste is lost in nine or twelve Months, by the Age of the Beer, and the Strength of the great Quantity of Hops that were used in its Preservation.

From here on, Ellis turned to discuss the properties of individual types of wood. The two most commonly used varieties of tree were oak and beech, and—as we describe subsequently in conjunction with discussions of the practices of some modern smoked-malt makers—aging the wood before use was common:

> There are many Maltsters where Wood is pleantiful that use this Fuel, as being the cheapest they can have for their Purpose, and is generally of but two Sorts, viz. The Oak and the Beech. The first, as it is of a very hard and durable Substance, they lay up in great Piles or Cocks to dry, and waste the sappy phlegmatic Part of the Wood, so that, when they come to use it, it will the sooner run into Fire, and consequently less Smoke, whererby the Tang or Vapour of it does the less Harm to the Malt. And so careful are they in this respect, that some will keep the Oak Sort seven or ten Years by them before they use it. But as the Beech is a Wood that much sooner decays, they only pile it abroad one Year, and take it into the Malt-house next, so that two Years fit this for Use. And to make it answer better, many in the Western Parts burn Coak with this, or Oak, and thus make it run sooner into a clear Fire, and less into Smoke. (p. 175)

Ellis later elaborated on the necessity of aging. Just to be sure we're all on the same page here, please note that a *billet* is a thick piece of wood cut to a suitable length for use as fuel.

> Beechen Billet, if laid abroad in a Stack, the first Year, and housed the second will burn with little Smoke. Oaken Wood smokes and blacks the Malt, but by several Years lying abroad in a Stack, the Sap will be wasted and do less Damage. (p. 256)

Of course there is always the contrarian view—whether given in earnest or in jest:

> Now they say, that such greenish Wood is beyond old Wood for this Purpose, because it burns stronger, drives off the Smoke quicker, gives a Gloss to the Malt, and a paler Colour and brisker Taste to the Drink; by Reason old Wood is longer burning, the Smoke weaker and stays the longer with the Malt. This Notion is contrary to the Warminster Maltsters as I have observed. (p. 321)

One final sort of tree is mentioned, the elm (p. 257): "There is such a disagreeable Sulphur in Elm, that the Smoke of it is very pernicious, if employ'd in drying Malt, and therefore it is every where rejected."

Ellis further reported that those trying to balance the benefits of coal with the economy of wood struck upon several schemes by which the two might be used together in some way (as we have already mentioned in another context):

> At Beasonsfield I have tasted a tolerable good common Ale, brewed with a Mixture of six Bushels of pale Malt, dried with Coak, and seven Bushels of brown, dried with Beech Wood. Others again, will dry a light Amber Malt, with some Coak, and some beechen Billet-Wood burnt together, and of this I have drank good Butt-Beer at Newbury; others burn Welch Coal and Wood tegether. (p. 255)

Beyond wood and straw, it appears that some maltsters also routinely resorted to other kinds of vegetation for fuel. Two that Ellis mentioned are fern and furz. Of the former,

> Drying malt with Fern at N———n, in Bucks— ——— Here the Maltster says, the best Way of all others to make this strong Fuel a mild, gentle sweet Sort is, to let such Fern have a good Shower of Rain on it after it is cut or mowed down, if he stays two

> or three Weeks for it, and then make it like Hay till it is very dry. (p. 321)

Now "furz" or "furze" may be as new to some readers as it was to us, so here's what the *Compact Edition of the Oxford English Dictionary* says: "The popular name of *Ulex europeus*, a spiny evergreen shrub with yellow flowers, growing abundantly on wastelands throughout Europe. Also named gorse, whin." Okay, so it was an evergreen shrub—maybe the origin of the term "fir" as a general description for evergreens. In any case, here's what the *London and Country Brewer* has to say about the stuff as fuel (p. 256): "Furz is too fierce a Fire, and its Stalks, being large, retain a considerable Deal of Sap, which renders it of ill Consequence to the Malt."

And finally, we have these brief but tantalizing mentions of some other odd fuels (p. 256): "In some Places they dry Malt with Peat, and, at a certain Town, a Person had a Contrivance to dry with Burnt Clay, without Smoke."

Although modern Scottish brewers seem generally to reject the premise that peat-smoked malt might ever have been used in beer, this passage gives some historical precedent for those who choose to brew with peated malt.

The burning of clay, on the other hand, might best be allocated to the alchemist's bag of imagined tricks.

Snuffed

The art, science, and commerce of brewing all advanced dramatically during the last half of the eighteenth century. Unfortunately, the effect of these advances on the subject of our current consideration—namely, smoke flavor in beer—was rather pejorative. Although maltsters continued to use wood to some degree as a fuel throughout the nineteenth century, it is clear that by 1820, smoke flavor was rapidly disappearing from British beer if, in fact, it was not already gone.

Through the period that we have reviewed thus far (to the mid-1700s), porter was made from a grist that was all brown malt. Thus any smoke character present in the malt would have certainly been conveyed to the finished beverage. And to be sure, Mr. Ellis has let us know that this often occurred. Indeed, it seems unlikely that porter could have been made *without* smoke flavor during this time, as it was routinely made from malt dried over wood, straw, or some other fibrous fuel.

But two things happened to reduce the smokiness of porter between 1780 and 1820. First, the smoke flavor of brown malts themselves most likely declined as production methods changed. Second, brewers began to substitute pale malt for brown malt, removing the smoky component from the grist. Let's look at these two phenomena.

In the mid-1700s brown malt was dried entirely over a roaring wood fire. But this practice appears to have changed as the use of coal and coke became generally accepted by all maltsters. A text published in 1798 (Hughes, 1798, p. 10) explains the

> real and necessary mode of drying high coloured amber, or porter malt....
>
> The best mode for drying malt for porter, is, to first harden your malt, this is, with a slow fire nearly half dry them, then...lay this half dryed, or hardened malt in a heap, 'til the next morning....
>
> The malt for snapping, should not be more than one inch and a half thick on the kiln; make a brisk fire with dry wood, and keep your malt continually turning, on the kiln; from a brisk fire the malt will

> snap; that is, the rind will burst, when you suppose that nearly the whole is snapped, draw your fire, and shift your kiln.

This method—where the brown or amber malt is dried first and then subsequently roasted over a wood fire—is consistently described in the malting literature from all parts of the nineteenth century (Roberts, 1847, p. 200; Levesque, 1853, p. 21; Tizzard, 1857, p. 85; Byrn, 1860, p. 139). The earliest description of the process suggests that the initial drying would have been conducted over a fuel other than wood, and subsequent authors give the same impression. Finally, the definitive work on malting by Stopes (1885, p. 161) makes this practice explicit:

> The fire may be of a moderate warmth of coke or anthracite coal, until the moisture is dissipated. Then the heat can be very largely augmented, and if a good quantity of billet-wood is thrown upon the fire, the result is the better.

The final factor to consider in this "improved" process for making brown and amber malts is that the roasting itself goes very quickly—one source says 1½ to 2 hours for brown malt.

When all of these factors are considered together, it appears that the brown and amber malts made during the nineteenth century would have had very little smoke character. First, dry, well-seasoned woods were used when the roasting was done. These woods are specified precisely because they give little smoke—a fact that is demonstrated in current commercial practice. Second, the malts were already dry when exposed to the smoke. Because many smoke components are water soluble, smoke flavors are not readily imparted to dry malt. And finally, the contact time between the smoke and the malt was fairly short—certainly 2 hours or less. In light of all the other factors, it seems highly unlikely that much smoke flavor would have been imparted to the malt during this short exposure.

As a result of these factors, we can only conclude that the smoke character of brown and amber malts declined significantly between 1750 and 1800. Although the malts themselves may still have had some smoke flavor when tasted directly, their impact on the flavor of the finished beer must have been dramatically reduced. Furthermore, brown malts were no longer the sole malt used in making porter. To make matters worse, the ability of brown malt to flavor the finished beer would decline further as the proportion of brown malt in porter recipes decreased.

Economics of Brown and Pale

The production of pale malt over coal or coke-fired kilns began in the early 1700s (Mathias, 1959, p. 6–7), and we have seen that this practice was widely accepted by the time that William Ellis wrote *London and Country Brewer*. The smoke flavor that remained in malts came from those dried by other fuels, most especially the brown malt used for making porter.

Smoky or otherwise, porter was hugely popular during the seventeenth century. The breweries that arose to produce this beer ranked among the largest industrial undertakings in all of Britain. And with such scale came a scrupulous attention to the economics of the business venture. Any savings realized in the production of the product paid handsome rewards to the owners of these breweries.

So it was that brown malt lost its place of pride in the making of porter. When John Richardson's treatise on the hydrometer, first published in 1785 (later updated: Richardson, 1788, p. 161), made clear to porter brewers that they could get 30 percent more extract from pale malts than from brown, the tide began to turn. Within a few years, pale malt composed a part of every porter grist.

This substitution of pale for brown malt might have been complete, except for one complication. Then as now, most consumers associated the deep color of a beer with its alcoholic strength. When brown malt came out of the grist, so did its color. And no one wanted to buy a pale porter, no matter what it tasted like.

A malt roaster with a direct fired roasting drum patented by Daniel Wheeler 1818.

To cover their increasing use of pale malt, porter brewers needed something to help them sustain the impression of alcoholic strength. In fact, through several decades in the late 1700s and early 1800s, they devised or discovered a number of substances to help out in this regard. On the benign side, they did things like burn sugar or molasses and added it to the kettle. On the more insidious side, they added things like strychnine, opium, and hemp to help give the beer a "kick" and ensure that folks would wake up in the morning feeling like they had gotten their money's worth (Daniels, 1996, p. 268).

This problem was finally solved in 1818 when Daniel Wheeler invented and patented the roasting drum for the production of black "patent" malt. Here, finally, was a malt that contained so much color that only a small amount was needed to bring the familiar porter color to a pale malt grist. From this point forward, brown malt—and its cousin amber malt—would find less and less use in porter grists throughout the land.

One John Tuck basically concluded that porter had gone to hell in a handbasket:

> I have already observed, that the real flavour of porter, as originally drank, is completely lost; and this by pale malts being introduced. As the old practice will hardly be taken up, suffice it to say, our ancestors brewed porter entirely with high dried malt; while, in the present day, in many houses, high dried or blown malts are entirely omitted. (Tuck, 1822 [1995], p. 124)

We have no doubt that the "original flavour" to which Tuck referred is the smoky, brown-malt character of the early porters. This lament serves to inform us clearly of its loss. Tuck further bemoaned the "patent malt" that has taken over:

> This [patent] malt has but latterly come into use; since the act of parliament passed for prohibiting the use of colour made from sugar. I cannot consider this malt a good substitute, as it is mere colour, without any of the saccharine substance remaining. It is however, now generally used by the London Porter houses, who much discontinue blown malts, substituting amber, as by these means they procure a greater weight of saccharine matter; about a 30th part of the whole grist will be sufficient for colour. (Tuck, 1822 [1995], p. 48)

Although amber and brown malts constituted one-half to two-thirds of the grist in the recipes that Tuck suggested for his "home brewer" readers, he acknowledged that commercial practice was not nearly so generous. Commercial recipes published by Amsinck (1868) after the midpoint of the century show a range of values for brown malt in porters that runs from less than 10 percent to nearly 25 percent—all lacking amber malt and supplemented by black patent malt. In these proportions, a malt with so little smoke as brown malt had by then could not have provided anything more than a subtle suggestion of smoke—a faint addition to the malt complexity of the style.

As further evidence of the impotence of brown malt in dilution, we should remember William Ellis—our smoke-sensitive chronicler from the 1700s—who said that he had a "tolerable good common Ale" that was made from slightly more than half brown malt (Ellis, 1742, p. 255).

The other factor that suggests the disappearance of smoke from beer is its disappearance from the discussions of maltsters and brewers. Whereas the literature before 1775 yields numerous references to smoke in malt or beer, we find no mention of "smoke" in the nineteenth century British brewing literature. By contrast, the German brewing literature of the same period covered it frequently, as we discuss later.

Finally, we have commentary from several sources who found that the utterly smokeless "patent" malt conveys the same flavor qualities as the torrified brown malt used for making porter and known as "blown malt": "Blown malts are now comparatively but little used; they are generally made of the worst barleys, and although bought at a much lower price, are very unproductive. "*Both colour and flavour can now be given quite as well with the best roasted malt.*" (Black, 1849, p. 29; emphasis added.) No wonder then, that Stopes (1885, p. 130) concluded: "Blown, brown or porter malt, is also differently prepared. Its use is an absurdity fast dying out."

Of course, porter was itself quite weak during the 1800s, and consumption plummeted as consumers switched to pale ales as the beverage of choice. Historian Peter Mathias (1959, p. 12) stated it succinctly: "Porter triumphed in the eighteenth century. The nineteenth century proved to be the century of ale, with the porter brewers forced to respond to the trend themselves either later or sooner." As a result of this change in consumer tastes, porter—with smoke flavor or without it—was on its way to obscurity.

With the removal of smoke from porter and the decline of porter overall, we lose nearly all traces of smoke in the beers of Britain. Clearly, the notoriously smoky fuels such as furze, fern, and green wood had been drummed out of the system by the time that Wheeler invented his patented roasting machine. Perhaps our only remaining hope that some smoke flavor might be conveyed to beer would be through a beer made largely from amber malt. Sadly, we find no evidence that this happy event occurred once "patent" malt arrived on the scene.

Thus we bring to a close our look at the history of smoke in British beers. We conclude that the flavor we're so fond of was found commonly in porters and other brown beers through most of the eighteenth century. Like many good things, its decline was hastened by technology. Changes in malt-making procedures reduced the smokiness of brown and amber malts; the invention of black "patent" malt nearly eliminated their use altogether. As porter passed from favor, the last vestiges of smoke flavor in British beer disappeared from the scene. And as best we can tell, it has not returned in any notable way since.

Smoked Malts in Germany

Tracking the course of brewing technology in Germany is not quite so easy as for Britain owing both to the language barrier and the much smaller collection of research literature of any type to be found in the United States. For this project, we were able to dip into the brewing library at the famous Weihenstephan Institute near Munich. Here we found enough literature to inform us of the basic course of smoke in malt among German brewers during the period of interest, namely, the eighteenth and nineteenth centuries.

Our survey of this literature leads us to several conclusions on the differences between kilning practices in Germany and those in Britain. First, German brewers generally malted their own barley, unlike British brewers who commonly purchased malt from a supplier. Second, air drying was apparently used to some significant extent as it is mentioned in several sources. Third, the adoption of coal lagged considerably behind the time frame in Britain, but when coal came, it was more quickly taken up by a majority of brewers. Let us consider each of these points in turn.

The combination of malting and brewing under a single roof has numerous implications for the production of malt. Under these circumstances, the malt is produced with an eye to how it will be used, and its production is considered to be an essential step in creating the flavor of the finished beer. Thus the maltster-brewer is unlikely to do anything in the production of malt that would have a pejorative effect on the final beer. In this context, we find little mention of fuels other than wood until the appearance of coal and coke.

Yet despite the lack of fuel alternatives, German brewers still managed to produce pale malts. In the late 1700s, we find sources that explain the differences between white beer and brown beer. They tell us clearly that brown beer was made from fully kilned malt and that white beer was made from air-dried, or perhaps only lightly kilned malts (Krüniß, 1784, p. 8; von Canerin, 1791, p. 8).

Here, as in Britain in the eighteenth century, smoke was an unwelcome element in beer, at least by some. According to one author, "The smoke from the fire must be kept completely away from the malt . . . but without it, the usefulness of the heat is lost" (Krüniß, 1784, p. 64). It is interesting that we also found some positive commentary on the subject:

> It is beer and here normal that one gets the smoke with the malt because the alkaline and burnt portions not only help the ground malt by improving the dissolution and extraction but also give the beer a more brown color and a warm expression. (von Canerin, 1791, p. 59)

Surely this "warm expression" is the positive flavor of smoke we all love.

Although these authors clearly distinguish between white beers made with air-dried malts and brown beers made from kilned malts, we also find mention of beers brewed from a mixture of both types, "to achieve a perfect balance" (Simon, 1803, p. 102–103).

So here's the question: If air-dried malts were so highly regarded, why kiln at all? The answer comes in simple logistics as the following passages indicate:

> Who so much room in their building has, that they can let their malt stand in the air to dry, will have good, pure, wine-colored beer. [German wines being, of course, white!] . . . .
>
> In winter you can't make air-malt because a little frost can destroy it, you must take refuge with a fire in the kiln. (Seifert, 1818 [1992, p. 9])

Thus limitations in space and the demands of the seasons drove brewers to make wood-kilned malt on a regular basis well into the 1800s. It is not until 1838 that we find the first reference to indirect heating for the production of malt. In this year, we find a source that talks about three types of kilns: *rauch* (smoke), *luft* (air), and *dampf* (steam). The first is a traditional direct-fired kiln; the second indirect, in which no combustion products touch the grains; and the last an indirect kiln heated by steam pipes.

Steam-heated kilns made a brief appearance in the British literature as well, but there as in Germany, the need for such a design was eliminated by the development of effective indirect kilning designs and the adoption of coal and coke as smokeless fuels for the *Rauchdarr* or smoke kiln.

The *Luftdarr* or air kiln was destined to dominate malting practice in Germany well before the close of the nineteenth century. It included duct work to keep the smoke of the fire away from the malt, while still transferring the heat needed to do the drying and roasting. Indeed, we found a report that the air kiln could "make malt that is black-brown, half-brown, light-brown and completely light without needing much wood" (Anonymous, 1838, p. 133).

Weihenstephan Institute's renowned Professor Narziss reviewed the history of nineteenth century malting and concluded that by 1860, these indirect kilns were coming into prominence in Germany. Furthermore, the remaining smoke kilns were being fueled by coke except in cases where beechwood was being used intentionally to produce a smoke-flavored malt (Narziss, 1986). Here, as with an earlier German reference (von Canerin, 1791, p. 59), we see smoke addressed as something that was at least potentially desirable as a component of beer flavor. Still, this is a modern reference, given with the knowledge that rauch malt has survived through the centuries and still commands a loyal following to this day. Other authors acknowledged the continued existence of smoke kilns during the late 1800s, but they offered little support for their survival.

According to one source from this period, "the number of followers for these [smoked] beers is small and therefore one actually only sees smoke kilns very occasionally and only in smaller breweries" (Leyser, 1893, p. 251). And Julius Thausing—the best-known chronicler of German brewing in the late 1800s—reported, "The smoke kiln has for us only historical interest. . . . Only a few are found in small breweries" (Thausing, 1898, p. 405).

Yet despite this faint praise for the glory of smoke in beer, the rare smoke kiln did survive, along with beers that clearly deliver smoked flavor. Now that we have seen how most smoky malts disappeared from German brewing by the mid-1800s, let us move on to consider the history of individual beers styles that expressed smoked flavor at a time when it was clearly out of favor.

Historic Smoked Beers

Although we can document the brewing of dozens of smoke-flavored beers by looking at the modern beer market, history shows us only a handful of beers that expressed smoke flavor beyond the time when smoke was eliminated as a common flavor element in most malts.

Porter is a style that evidently expressed smoke flavor in its early days—and even during its height. But as we have seen, the smokiness of porter declined with the changes in, and reduction of, the brown malt used in its brewing. There is already a great deal of debate about the properties of porter (brown versus robust) at different times in its history. Now we can add to this debate the factor of smoke, which clearly seems to have a place in brown porter, but seems unlikely to have been evident in the later robust manifestation.

Not surprisingly, it is Germany—where we today find the only *surviving* (as opposed to recreated) commercial example of smoked beer—that also presents us with some purposely smoked beers from the past. Here, two specific styles deserve mention: Grätzer and Lichtenhainer.

Grätzer was popular in a number of cities in the area that is now Poland, "Provinz Posen und Westpreussen," a little more than 100 years ago. Between 1890 and 1900, five breweries in the city of Grätz (Grodzisk) alone produced 100,000 hectoliters (about 85,000 U.S. barrels) of this beer.

Grätzer derived its smoked flavor, not from smoked barley, but from smoked wheat (Schönfeld, 1938, p. 162). That fact alone makes it unique among the smoked beers we have examined, but one further feature makes it novel.

Rather than smoking with beech—the wood of choice for most German rauch beers, the Grätzer grains were smoked over oak as we saw with some British maltsters.

Historical accounts specify that the smoke flavor was achieved during a kilning that lasted 36 to 48 hours (Schönfeld, 1938, p. 162), and some modern sources indicate that the resulting wheat malt might have had a somewhat roasted character (Dawson, 1996). But details published when Grätzer was probably still being produced tell that the final kiln temperature was 122 to 133 °F (50 to 56 °C) (Wahl and Henius, 1908, p. 1280–1281), so the likely product was in fact very pale.

What we know for sure is that the beer was low in gravity and well hopped. The sources for this information come from 1908 and 1938—early enough for direct familiarity with the modern producers of the style; these sources tell us that the beer was brewed from a wort of original specific gravity (SG) 1.028 to 1.034 (7 to 8.5 °P). Even more remarkably, we find that the hopping rates were quite high—easily sufficient to deliver 30 to 35 IBUs.

One counterpoint to this high hop level would have been the relatively full body of the finished beer—perhaps as high as 1.012 SG (3 °P). This characteristic resulted from a high-temperature, infusion-mashed wort that was "protein rich and relatively dextrin free"

(Schönfeld, 1938, p. 163; see also Wahl and Henius, 1908). Furthermore, it was fermented with a highly flocculent, low-attenuation yeast.

Schönfeld (1938, p. 163) described Grätzer as having a "full, round, malty flavor" in which the smoke and hop bitterness were "intense." Wahl and Henius (1908, p. 1281) were more expressive: "The color of the beer is like that of Pilsener, and the taste is said to be deliciously tart and wine-like."

Lichtenhainer is another old German rauch beer (*rauchbier*) that employed smoked malt. It is described as a "pale, light [-bodied] sour beer" and is distinguished from Berliner weissbier through its use of barley rather than wheat. It appears that the wort was uncooked and minimally hopped so as not to hinder or delay the development of the desired souring. Unlike Grätzer, this style does not appear to have survived long enough to leave a contemporary record of its production.

Although these dead styles have historical interest for brewers and especially those of us interested in smoke-flavored beers, the key focus of our attention naturally falls upon the still thriving beers of Bamberg.

The brewing literature provides clear documentation of beer production in Bamberg through the last few centuries. We even found a book by Johann Albert Joseph Seifert titled *Das Bamberger Bier,* which appeared initially in 1818 and was republished recently (1992) by a Bamberg-based publisher. When we stumbled upon this thin volume, our hopes soared. But unfortunately, the book consumes its 85 pages without so much as a mention of "rauch" or smoke in any respect. It lauds Bamberger beer for "its nourishment, its mild taste, its clarity, its strong and intoxicating quality" (Seifert, 1818 [1992, p. iv]). But at the same time, it details the use of air-drying of malt and discusses the making of white beer from it, which would obviously have lacked smoke flavor. Still, it is clear that the Bamberg brewers made brown beer alongside the white through this period, and earlier sources (Krüniß, 1784, p. 20) confirm that the Bamberg brown was "dark brown and strong." Since brown malt would have come only from drying in a rauch kiln over a wood fire during this period, we can only conclude that these beers were the smoky ancestors of today's well-liked classics.

Despite the thin documentation of smoked-beer brewing in Bamberg from the beer literature, we have a strong sense that it has been continuous for several centuries. The two current Bamberg rauchbier breweries are owned by families that have been brewing beer in the same location for numerous generations. When asked, each will tell you that they have been making beer in the same manner—with beech-smoke malt—for as long as anyone can remember. Both breweries have long histories: Schlenkerla was established in 1678 and Spezial dates back to 1536.

Schlenkerla plays up its colorful history, noting that its name may designate someone who is limping or someone who is stumbling because of drink. Although the brewery is officially registered as "Heller Bräu" after an early family member, the brewery earned the "Schlenkerla" moniker in the late 1800s. It seems that the proprietor at the time walked with a bit of a limp.

A view of the full facade of the Schlenkerla gasthaus.

This trait earned him—and ultimately the brewery—an unusual name that has come to be known worldwide as a source of good beer.

As for the Spezial brewery, we know little more of its history, only that the current Merz family took the reins in 1898.

CHAPTER 2

Classic Producers of Smoke-Flavored Beers

The production of smoke-flavored beers does not require the application of brewing techniques beyond those already understood and practiced by brewers of various types of beer. To be sure, the making of a classic German Märzen is quite different from the process employed in producing a porter in the American style. But these differences relate generally to the production of ales and lagers and have no bearing on the application or inclusion of smoked malt flavor in the finished product.

Without a doubt, successful production of smoked beers depends on good smoked malt. Many of the brewers we surveyed, both here and abroad, rely on commercial maltsters to supply this essential ingredient. Still, a few brewers are either brave enough, stubborn enough, or perhaps particular enough to smoke their own malt—either as a process of malting itself or as a supplementary treatment to finished malt from a regular maltster.

In each case, these malt-smoking brewers use unique facilities as well as techniques that are rarely found outside their own operations. To help the reader better understand how classic producers generate the essential smoked malt, this chapter reviews malt preparation and brewing at three classic smoked-beer producers—the Schlenkerla and Spezial breweries in Bamberg, and the Alaskan Brewing Company in Juneau. In addition, we'll talk about the production of both beechwood- and peat-smoked malts (from Weyermann Specialty Malting Company of Bamberg and the Bairds Malting Company of Arbroath, Scotland, respectively) that are available to brewers in the United States.

Before we begin our discussion of the individual producers, a brief review of the malting process is in order. As most brewers know, malting converts raw barley into a form suitable for brewing. The process induces the barley seed to germinate and begin growing, just as it would when planted in the ground. The sequence of changes that takes place during this weeklong ordeal prepares both enzymes and starch for the brewer's use. Like brewing itself, the basic process of malting is simple, but the potential for variation makes it highly complex. There are three main steps.

Steeping: The barley is soaked in water for various periods until total moisture content approaches 50 percent.

Germination: The soaked barley is laid in a screen-bottomed bed or "box" that is ventilated to control temperature, oxygen, and humidity conditions. It is here that the nascent barley plant contained in each barley kernel begins to grow. During this phase, the roots will sprout and grow to several times the length of the kernel itself. To prevent entanglement of the roots and ensure consistent conditions in the box, the germinating barley must be mixed and turned several times each day.

Kilning: When germination reaches a desired point, the green malt is placed on or in a kiln for drying—and smoking if appropriate—and then for toasting. Time and temperature conditions are carefully controlled in order to achieve the desired character in the finished malt.

Now that we have reviewed malting, let us move on to discuss the practices of the classic producers of smoke-flavored beers.

Schlenkerla

The Schlenkerla Brewery was originally located at the site of the current-day *gasthaus*, in the oldest and most crowded part of Bamberg. But around 1930, the brewery's operations migrated to the current site of production a mile or so to the south in a part of Bamberg known as Stephansberg.

Perched on one of Bamberg's "seven hills," this compact facility includes everything needed to convert raw barley into packaged beer at the rate of 12,000 hectoliters (about 10,000 U.S. barrels) per year. That means not only malting, brewing, and packaging facilities, but also storage for most of the raw materials that feed the process. To understand, let us begin at the beginning, with malt.

Schlenkerla produces its own malt year-round. But anyone who has ever visited a malting plant would be surprised at the diminutive nature of Schlenkerla's malting facilities. At most maltings, germination boxes range from bowling-alley to football-field size. But at Schlenkerla, you could cover the germination box with a double-bed mattress.

At Schlenkerla, beechwood is protected from moisture and aged for a year or longer before being burned to produce the smoke that flavors the brewery's malt.

When it comes to malting, it is not the facilities that eat up real estate; it is the supplies. The brewery maintains grain silos for both barley and finished malt. Since the malt requires two to three months' aging after production, that means a considerable inventory of grain must be on hand at any one time. Despite this, the real space hog is not the grain, it's the wood.

In a courtyard at the rear of the brewery, visitors will find ten-foot-high piles of aging beechwood stacked in neat rows under a corrugated tin roof. The square footage consumed by this cache of timber easily exceeds that required for the combined steeping, germination, and kilning facilities indoors. But this stash is important. This is where the wood that stokes the kiln and smokes the grain spends many months in silent slumber. Once cut, the locally grown beechwood must age or season for one to two years before it's ready for use.

When it's time for service, the wood is thrown to the flames in a footlocker-sized firebox that vents directly to the 10 foot by 10 foot kiln. Although we did not discuss fire tending in detail, it was clear that the logs combust fully before burning down to coals. At Schlenkerla, this method seems consistent with the procedures used at the Weyermann Specialty Malting Company where Thomas Kraus-Weyermann explained to us that properly seasoned wood burns readily while producing almost no visible smoke. To prevent the formation of nitrosamines, sulfur is burned with the logs.

Traditional wooden beer barrels are still used for draft beer at the Schlenkerla and Spezial breweries in Bamberg.

At Schlenkerla, the brewing itself takes place in a brew house with a 50-hectoliter (42.5–U.S. barrel) capacity. A double-decoction mash is used. Hop extracts are added for bittering in the kettle, and our records show no mention of late-addition hops.

After knockout, the brewers chill, pitch, and aerate the wort and then separate trub by cold flotation in square-cornered, closed fermentation tanks. After a traditional fermentation at about 10 °C, the beers are lagered for six to eight weeks.

The lagering takes place in sandstone caverns below the brewery. An extensive network of caves and tunnels has existed underneath Bamberg for many centuries. At one time, nearly every brewery in town used them as a source of natural refrigeration, and every building was once connected to them. Today, Schlenkerla is the last brewer to use the caves, located nearly 40 feet below ground level. One can only imagine the logistical difficulties that must have been encountered while installing the 90-barrel lager tanks in the unforgiving stone rooms.

In addition to lagering, Schlenkerla carries out filtering and keg-filling activities in these subterranean cold rooms. Back above ground, they operate a bottling line rigged for the standard German half-liter returnable bottle. Here the bottle washer alone is as big as most bottling and labeling stations found in the United States.

Spezial

At the Spezial Brewery, we found an operation that was quite similar to that of Schlenkerla, but on a somewhat smaller scale. Their brewery is still located at the

Dry beechwood is loaded into the firebox for the malt kiln at Spezial.

back of the *gasthaus* where 85 percent of the beer is sold. Although Schlenkerla employs a number of people from outside the owner's family, including a professional brewmaster, beer at Spezial is still made by Christian Merz, the current proprietor descended from a long string of Merzes who have run Spezial.

Malting at Spezial uses a specially designed round unitank where steeping and germination can be carried out without transferring the grain. From there, the green malt goes to the kiln, which was perhaps eight feet by eight feet square. With this equipment, Herr Merz processes one batch of malt each week, and each load begins with 3000 kilograms (3.25 tons) of barley.

As at Schlenkerla, beechwood logs are well aged or seasoned before use—as long as three or four years according to Merz. He said the combination of dry wood and a low fire avoids problems with nitrosamines. The Spezial kiln employed a monitoring and control station that could be used to assess and adjust conditions in the kiln. The arrangement included screens between the firebox and the kiln floor to keep cinders and fly ash from getting to the malt. It also included dampers by which Merz can control the mix and volume of air to achieve optimal kilning conditions.

Kilning takes about 36 hours, and the finished malt is stored for six to eight weeks before use. The finished malt has the character and color of Munich malt.

Merz said that he malts only during the winter, both because the dry air is preferable for the smoking and because it is easier to maintain cool temperatures for germination. As a result of his seasonal production, Merz must vary the proportion of smoked malt in his recipes throughout the year because the smoke flavor diminishes with time. Depending on its potency, Merz said that he uses 40–60 percent rauch (i.e., smoked) malt in the Märzen recipe.

A room filled with smoked malt at the Spezial brewery in Bamberg.

In the 50-hectoliter (42.5–U.S. barrel) brew house, Spezial employs a double-decoction mash. Hopping is achieved with two hop charges employing two varieties of hops during the 65-minute boil. The fermentation and lagering regimen follows the usual lager beer temperatures, and lagering itself usually continues for six weeks. Total annual output is 7,000 hectoliters (about 6000 U.S. barrels).

Weyermann Beechwood Smoked Malt

Brewers in most parts of the world can acquire authentic Bamberg beechwood–smoked malt from the Weyermann Specialty Malting Company. This malt is kilned over a fire fueled with aged beechwood following procedures that are very similar to those of the two Bamberg breweries that make their own smoked malt.

To ensure that an appropriate smoked flavor is produced, Weyermann seasons the beechwood for 18 months or longer. Thomas Kraus-Weyermann told us that before using a batch of wood, he would test it in the household fireplace where it would burn "almost without any smoke at all." As was the case at Spezial, Weyermann does not appear to use phenol tests or other methods of chemical analysis to achieve the desired level of

The Weyermann Malt house steams during operations.

smokiness in the finished malt. Instead, the malting company insists that the primary quality-control feature is the taste of the finished malt.

The Weyermann malt is widely used by smoked-beer producers in and around Bamberg, and it has found favor with quite a number of American brewers as well. Because of its ready availability and predictable smoke flavor, many of the recipes in this book are based upon the Weyermann malt.

Quality and Consistency

As we have described, in the course of researching this book we talked to three makers of Bamberg smoked malt: Schlenkerla, Spezial, and Weyermann. In every case, we were interested not only in the actual procedures, but also in any techniques used to measure the amount of smoke flavor imparted to the malt and ensure consistency in the finished beer. In nearly every case, we were told that the taste of the finished product was the main, if not the only, measure by which the malt was assessed.

Still some further insights emerged. During an early visit at Schlenkerla, Ray was told that they sample the steam from the kiln and measure the amount of phenols present. But at Spezial, Merz said such tests were too expensive for practical use. Instead he relies on the taste of the malt, both directly and as the product of a Congress mash (a small, laboratory mash; the name comes from the European Brewing "Congress").

At Schlenkerla, the real key to consistency seemed to come not from the kilning, but from later steps in the process that effectively mix numerous batches of malt together in a single batch of finished beer. Each silo of finished malt consists of twelve individual kilnings. During brewing, they draw from two different silos for each batch of brew. Then, one fermentation tank takes two brews to fill, and a lager tank combines six different brews. As a result of this mixing, most of the batch-to-batch variations that might occur in the flavor of the smoked malt can be evened out.

Alaskan Smoked Porter—The History

Although the Old World gives us smoked beers produced by using methods that have long been established, the New World presents a "classic" smoked beer with a somewhat shorter history. We present that history through the lens of personal experience, as one of us, Geoff Larson, is the co-owner of Alaskan Brewing Company with his partner and wife, Marcy Larson.

Alaskan Brewing first produced its smoked porter in December 1988. It was released as a single batch, and it was called Chinook Alaskan Smoked Porter (*Chinook* was subsequently dropped from the name). The inspiration to produce a smoked porter came from historical research conducted by Marcy Larson on the breweries that were located in Alaska in the late 1800s and early 1900s.

Alaska was "The Last Frontier" in the westward expansion of the United States. It was also the final continental location of newly discovered gold in North America and thus was the site of the continuation of the westward gold rush. The population boom created by the gold seekers fostered a rewarding but challenging location to brew beer.

While researching turn-of-the-century breweries, Marcy was assisted by historians, librarians, and collectors who provided all sorts of information. This research yielded advertisements and newspaper interviews of the brewers that told a great deal about the materials and procedures. The resourceful brewers of early Alaska were forced to contend with extreme weather and difficult logistics to produce the beer desired by the thirsty gold seekers.

Brewers and miners alike were familiar with the popular styles of the time, and the brewers tried to satisfy their customers with similar fare. One 1898 advertisement

R.N. De Armond Collection, Alaska State Library

In Alaska many breweries malted their grain just as the Juneau Alaska Brewing and Malting Company did. Here the Juneau brewery is advertising its Porter in a late 19th century advertisement.

from the Juneau Alaska Brewing and Malting Company promoted porter. During this time, some breweries were kilning their own malt—probably because of the limited availability of colored malts. It was this history of porter production in Alaska—including the use of locally kilned malt which likely had smoky roasted characters—that planted the idea for the product now known as Alaskan Smoked Porter.

In 1986, Geoff and Marcy Larson had established their new brewery in Juneau, across the street from a newly opened salmon-smoking operation called Taku Smokeries. This coincidence markedly contributed to the development of Alaskan Smoked Porter. Within a few years of their respective startups, it became a sort of tradition on Friday afternoons for Sandro Lane, proprietor of Taku Smokeries, to bring some fresh smoked fish over to the Alaskan Brewery to be enjoyed with some freshly brewed beer while the two groups compared the week's work. Unfortunately, Alaskan's flagship amber beer became more of a thirst quencher for this event than a food accompaniment, because of the strong flavors of the smoked fish. After sampling the delicious but assertive tastes of the smoked fish, the beer flavor all but vanished. Geoff and company soon knew they needed a bigger beer for the Friday afternoon gatherings, and talk of the historically brewed porters came up. The thought that most colored malts made in early Juneau were direct-fire kilned led naturally to pairing smoke and porter.

To produce a modern porter similar to that brewed a hundred years earlier in Juneau, Alaskan Brewery used the Taku Smokeries smokehouse. Work began by smoking malt for a porter recipe that then–Alaskan brewer John Maier had developed. (Maier later moved on to become Brewmaster at Rogue Brewing located in Newport, Oregon.) Geoff collaborated with Sandro Lane on the malt smoking. They tried hot-smoking and cold-smoking methods and finally settled on a smoking program that blended elements of both. They discovered that balancing the intense flavors of alderwood smoke

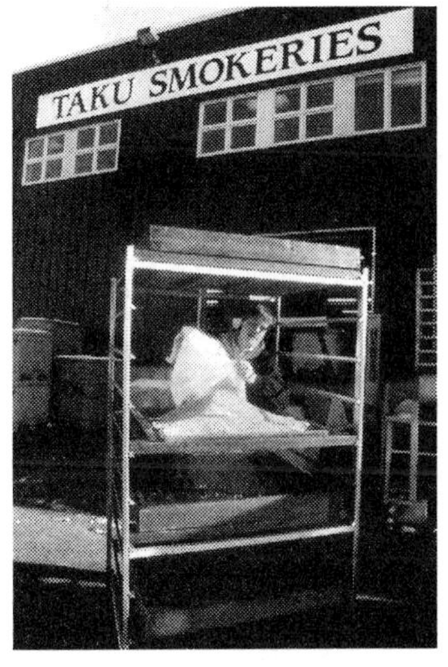

Geoff Larson layering the grain on trays in front of Taku Smokeries.

Hot and Cold Smoking

Hot smoking allows higher-temperature smoke into the smoke house and tends to create more of the sharp, acrid flavors in the malt. Cold smoking allows much cooler smoke into the smokehouse, which imparts a more delicate and woody smoke aroma and flavor to the malt.

In professional smoking operations, lox is made by a cold-smoking technique that slowly dries but does not cook the salmon while it is smoked. The hot-smoking technique, on the other hand, does cook the salmon as it is smoked.

with those of the beer was best achieved by using predominately a cold-smoking technique.

Use of a commercial smoking facility allows total control of the smoking process. The parameters controlled include temperature, humidity, gas velocity, and smoke density. Through manipulation of these variables, smoke can be generated in a manner that is safe for foodstuffs and delivered in a way that maximizes the positive flavor elements of the smoke in the malt.

In this process, Alaskan uses wet alderwood with controlled airflow and low temperatures of combustion. The smoke generator is remote from the smokehouse, and the smoke thus provided is cool. The smoke is transported to the malt through baffled conduits that filter out potentially hazardous ash and cinder particles. Moistened malt is spread on copper and stainless steel screen racks that are then placed in the smokehouse. The malt is smoked and then dried at elevated temperatures that darken the malt slightly.

Geoff Larson pushing the smoking racks into the smoke house at Taku Smokeries.

In 1993, they started to leave a small amount of yeast in the bottled beer, brewed the beer slightly stronger, and began to suggest aging of the beer to consumers.

Geoff tasting the malt's progress during the smoking operations.

Since discovery of the aging potential of smoked porter, the Alaskan Brewery has kept a journal library of each year's brew. In the first year, the smoke character mellows substantially while the hop's aromatic profile becomes more subdued. In the second year, bitterness diminishes enough to let the chocolate flavors step to the forefront, where they combine with the malt sweetness to lend a toffee-like character to the beer. After the third year, the smoke has stepped back, almost becoming a secondary flavor component. At this point, some overtones like dried fruit and sherry also develop as would be expected with older ales and barley wines. After four years, the sherrylike characters dominate the flavor profile of the smoked beer. During the fifth and sixth years of aging, the smoke appears to come back to the forefront as a very complex, more woody, caramel-like flavor. By this time, the beer is more subtle in its complexity; however, this is what allows the smoke flavors to reemerge to center stage of the smoked porter's flavor profile.

Peat Reek

Reek is the Scottish word for *smoke*. And peat-smoked malt from the Bairds Malting Company is one of the two types of smoked malt commercially available to brewers in the United States and elsewhere.

Geoff visited Arbroath, Scotland, to witness the Bairds Malting Company as it was starting up a new facility for making malt using peat reek. This facility is replacing the one in Pencaitland where the neighbors are not as accommodating to the traditional peat reek emanating from the facilities.

Peat is widely used as a fuel source in Scotland and Ireland, where wood is at a premium. Peat is actually the remains of plants like heather and sphagnum moss, which have accumulated over thousands of years. These remains become hard packed into a moist woody mass that—given enough pressure, temperature, and time—would become coal. Peat is harvested from these herbaceous deposits or "peat bogs" that are found throughout the United Kingdom. Peat-smoked—called "peated"—malt is most commonly used by distillers in making Scotch whisky.

Traditionally when malt was manufactured on site in Scotland, the fuel used in the kilning process was peat together with any other fuels readily available. The peat source worked very well because when the weather was too warm for malting in the spring and summer, the workers from the malt houses were employed digging the peat. These men would cut and then raise the peat chunks above ground to let them dry in preparation for the autumn and winter when malting would shift into full production, requiring this significant fuel source for the kilning of the green (wet) malt (Pigott, 1980, p. 50).

The peated malting process at Arbroath is essentially the same as is used for making pale malt up to the later stages of kilning. When the malt is dried in the kiln to a level of 12 percent moisture, the process for peat-smoked malt diverges from regular pale malt. It is at this stage that the malt is trucked to a farm facility outside of town, where the drying is then completed by heat generated from burning peat. This process is carried out in the country as the burning of damp peat generates tremendous amounts of smoke with a sharp creosote smell. In this direct fire where nitrous oxides can form, elemental sulfur is burned to assure that nitrosamine levels will be under 5 parts per billion. It takes 5 days for this malt to pick up the desired peat-smoke characters, and by the end of this part of the process, the moisture level has been lowered to the desired 4 percent.

In the Pencaitland operation, the Bairds Malting Company starts the peat smoking at the 28 percent moisture level. Because of the higher moisture level, it only takes two days to attain the desired peated character at this facility. Hugh Baird representatives noted that a close approximation of peat-smoked malt can also be made by simply rewetting pale malt and drying it over a peat fire.

The company is analytically focused on the production of their smoked malt as they supply many different distillers with peated malt for many famous brands of Scotch whisky. Each distiller will specify the level of phenols they want in their malt. In their production of peated malt, Hugh Baird maltsters target 60 ppm phenol in each batch of malt and then blend it to the levels desired by their customers.

Hugh Baird peat-smoked malt is currently available in the United States for brewing beer, and it is supplied at high (13–20 ppm), medium (7–12 ppm), and low (4–6 ppm) phenol levels. This malt is very distinctive and assertive and can easily dominate a beer's flavor profile. It is best to use the peated malts for big, rich malty ales (strong scotch ales—also known as wee heavy—or barley wines, for example) because of peat's earthy and tangy flavor. It is best to limit its use in beer formulations as a secondary flavor component and then work up from there. Medium and low phenolic malts are readily available.

CHAPTER 3

Smoke Around the World

Despite the relative paucity of smoked beers, nearly every beer competition—homebrew or professional—has a category for them. These categories typically include two subgroups: *Bamberg-Style Rauchbier* and *All Other Smoked Beers*. We'll start this chapter with a quick look at what to expect in smoked beers in general and then move on to take an up-close look at smoked beers of the world—from Atlanta to Anchorage.

Smoke Defined

The range of flavor possible from smoke is incredibly wide. Yet despite this, traditional smoking and modern practice have settled on some similar woods: beechwood comes first, and oak is a distant second. Other woods, such as Alaskan's alder, have been used with great success, and these days peat-smoked malt has some ardent supporters as well.

Each of these smoke sources has unique characteristics, special aromas and flavors that betray their identity. And yet, when we transfer smoke to malt and subsequently to beer, we don't always get those special flavors that we want. Although wood smoke can provide a rich woody character, we have also seen it impart a piercing phenolic note. Smoking can create malt with a pleasant toasted flavor, but it can also result in burnt, charred notes that do little to enliven a beer. And smoking can convey pleasant baconlike or hamlike richness; however, it can also produce a rubbery, sulfurous stench.

To further complicate matters, American brewers have applied their creative genius and come up with many different juxtapositions of smoke and beer. Porter is certainly a favored style, and *wee heavy* is too. But that's not to stop people from adding smoke to bocks and doppelbocks, brown ales, dunkels, barley wines, weizens, kölsches, and even a Pilsener or two. Furthermore, they may juxtapose smoke flavor with other elements such as chili peppers, oak aging, or lactic fermentation.

Thus the flavors that you find when you pick up a smoked beer may vary quite widely. If you are buying a smoked beer—or judging one—very few labels or style designations can help you prepare for the actual flavor that you'll get when you pick up the glass. Still, nearly all are pleasant and enjoyable, and nearly every session with a smoked beer ends with a final satisfied sip from the new discovery. And that's what makes tasting smoked beer so much fun!

Whether you are buying smoked beers or judging them, there a few types that you can expect to run into. Here's how we describe them.

The Bamberg style is based on the German Märzen lager style. As a result, it is malty, amber, and smooth. On the basis of the classic producers in Bamberg, the smoke flavor in these beers may be strong or light, but it is always based on beechwood with a rich woody character that is discernible in the aroma and clearly displayed upon first tasting the beer. Sharp phenolic notes, burnt character, and other unpleasant flavors should be absent. In addition to the Märzen style, Bamberg brewers make other smoked lagers in the dunkel and bock styles. These present a similar richness of wood-smoke flavor, integrated with the classic character of these styles.

Because beechwood-smoked malt is available to home and commercial brewers in the United States and many other countries, you'll often find this character in smoked beers produced outside Bamberg as well. Here the smoke intensity may vary according to the wishes of the brewer, but the flavor should still include the pleasant woody notes found in the Bamberg classics. Indeed, thanks to American brewers, these malts have found their way into a wide range of beers that we discuss later in this chapter.

Perhaps the next most popular smoked malt is that with a Scottish peat reek. Peat-smoked malts, diverted from the supplies destined for Scotch distillers, have found their way to America where they have been brewed into a diverse range of beers. Chief among these are the Scotch and Scottish ale styles. Especially in the big and complex wee heavy, a touch of peat smoke can be an enticing addition. One of us—Ray—remembers judging a homebrewed doppelbock from the second round of the 1999 National Homebrew Competition where the peat was expressed with a full earthy flavor to provide an attractive enhancement. These effects are accomplished through very small additions of peat-smoked malt—often

1 percent is enough to do the job. Too much though, and the flavor shifts from the pleasant earthy tones to a piercing phenol note that few find inviting.

Finally, we have all other smoked malts. Many brewers live in areas where unique indigenous hardwoods can be found. Use of these woods in the making of smoked malt can lead to a pleasant and enjoyable novelty that might win you awards or even help you launch a brewery. But for those who are trying a new smoked beer in this category for the first time, there may be little information to guide your expectations. Here you get to drink, savor, and enjoy the rich new distribution of smoke flavors that can come from an unfamiliar wood.

Tasting Smoked Beers

Before we start describing the commercial examples of smoked beers that we have sampled in recent years, we should make a few comments about tasting and smoke.

Smoke is an intense flavor agent—even when present in small amounts. As a result of that intensity, your palate tends to react strongly to it initially: you take the first taste, and your mouth tells you, "Wow! That's smoky!" But another feature of that intensity is taste adaptation. After you've had three to six swallows of smoked beer—

especially if you are drinking it alone without food—you'll find that the smoke flavor is dramatically diminished. Thus beers with a relatively light smoke character often seem to lose their smoke flavor as you drink. Only those with a stronger presentation will hold on through a pint to give a steady—although still diminished—presentation of smoke flavor.

Of course, the problem with the "strong" approach is that many folks who try a sip of such a beer won't come back for a second taste—it simply blows them away. Thus commercial brewers tend to make subtly smoked beers that don't get returned upon first sip. Homebrewers, on the other hand, tend to crank up the smoke so that they can be sure it will still be asserting itself during the second or third pint of the night.

Both of these cases present problems for judges. When judging a sequence of beers, your palate only gets one shot at that "first beer" taste. After that, adaptation sets in, and your ability to detect smoke is considerably reduced. In commercial judging where all the beers in a flight are presented simultaneously, one of us—again, Ray—has recently addressed this issue by first smelling all the beers and recording comments about their aromas. During this process, he notes the smoke intensity of each beer. Then, when it is time to start tasting, he tastes the beers in order from least smoky to most smoky. Although this approach would not entirely prevent adaptation of your palate to smoke flavor, it does keep you from tasting a hugely smoky beer right off the bat and then being insensitive to the more subtle smokiness of the remaining beers.

When judging homebrews, there is currently no way to get around this dilemma. Each beer is presented separately, then tasted and scored before moving on to the next. The only possible solution might be the use of some "smoke intensity" scale on the part of the brewers, similar to the "sweet/medium/dry" scale used by mead makers. With such a scale, brewers could specify their beer as having low, medium, or high smoke intensity and help the judges to taste them in the proper order.

After our experiences in tasting smoked beer in the United States, we made an effort to try each of the Bamberg beers with a clean palate. Of course, this approach required that we spend more time in Bamberg and thereby drink even more *rauchbier* (smoked beer) overall, but somehow the sacrifice was worth it. Just remember that if you are tasting more than one smoked beer in a single setting, start with the beer with the lightest smoke character and work up from there.

Okay, with these preliminaries taken care of, let's start our tour of smoked beers. We'll start off with the German examples—found almost exclusively in and around Bamberg—then move on to consider the American scene. To wrap things up, we'll mention one or two other beers that fall outside these camps.

The Beers of Bamberg

The town of Bamberg lies astride two rivers in the rolling hills of Franconia in northern Bavaria. Like many German towns, it has kept up with modern technology without losing the inherent charm of rustic German culture. Thus ads for Internet service providers beckon from glass and steel kiosks set in front of white-washed plaster residences that were built not long after Columbus sailed the ocean blue.

A stroll through Bamberg's oldest streets reveals cozy lodgings, purveyors of fine antiques, and—to the beer drinker's delight—a clutch of classic German *gasthaus* breweries.

Inside these authentically ancient halls, one finds the usual mix of German *gemütlichkeit*, gastronomy, and grog. But here in Bamberg, the beer drinker also finds a rare gem of the beer world: that barbecued bastion of brew known as *rauch beer* or *rauchbier*.

Rauch means *smoke* in German, and for the casual foreign observer of the German language, it is a word usually associated with the consumption of tobacco products. But in Bamberg, "rauch" opens up a new world of beer flavor—one rooted long in the past and sustained by a culture that is at once enduring and adaptable.

The smoke-flavored beers of Bamberg derive their flavor from an ingredient made famous by America's biggest brewer, namely beechwood. In the Anheuser-Busch breweries, beechwood chips play only a passive role as a sterilized support medium for indolent yeast cells. But in Bamberg, as we have described, the wood gives its all for a much more direct flavor impact. Here, whole beechwood logs are aged to perfection under covered storage areas and then burned under a bed of wet, green malt in order to infuse a distinctive wood-smoke flavor into the finished brewing grains.

Unlike some specialties that can be traced to but a single beer or brewery, rauchbier is a regional offering produced in myriad interpretations. These range from the dark brown and assertively smoked Aecht Schlenkerla rauch beer to the pale and Pilsenerlike Hartmann brewery Felsentrunk, which displays just a hint of smoke.

The classic Bamberg rauchbier is based on the Märzen or Oktoberfest style: a malty, amber beer with 4 to 4.8 percent alcohol by weight (5 to 6 percent by volume). But among the many breweries in the Bamberg area, a range of other beer styles will be found with smoke flavor including bock, doppelbock, schwarz (or black) beer, dunkel, and even a wheat-based weizen or two.

Many of the modern smoked-beer brewers in Franconia purchase malt from Weyermann Specialty Malting Company located just north of the train station on the east side of Bamberg. But the two best-known rauchbiers come from long-time producers who still make their own malt as well as their own beer. Let's begin our look at German rauchbier with visits to these two prototypical producers, Schlenkerla and Spezial.

Homegrown Smoke

Among the nine breweries of Bamberg, Schlenkerla and Spezial specialize in the production of smoke-flavored beers. Like most small brewers in Germany, both are family owned and have been for many generations. Both operate a *gasthaus* with lodgings above and the restaurant and bar downstairs. Here the beers are served in the traditional fashion "*vom fass*," which means draft

The range of smoke-flavored beers produced by Bamberg's two best-known rauchbier brewers, Spezial and Schlenkerla.

straight from the barrel. In both cases, their stories stretch back so far that their founding dates precede most salient events of American history. Yet despite the similarities, the two are quite different—both in the character of their beers and in the conduct of their business.

In both respects, Schlenkerla comes across as the bolder of the two. Schlenkerla's assertively smoked beers seem to draw tourists and locals in equal numbers to their tavern on a narrow cobbled street in the shadow of Bamberg's famous Dom cathedral. Their play for the tourist market is evident not only from the attractive selection of postcards and logo-imprinted glasses and

Here Spezial on Obere Konigstrasse is in the process of loading their delivery truck parked in front of the Gasthaus. A Gasthaus is a brewery, restaurant and hotel.

steins sold on site, but also from the fact that you can find these same souvenirs at other shops in the much-visited *altstadt* (old city).

Spezial, on the other hand, seems more a part of workaday Bamberg. Their beers carry a modest but still obvious smoke character that may better lend itself to everyday consumption. Situated just northeast of the Main-Donau Canal on the busy Obere Königstrasse, their tavern seems to attract a local clientele. Here you will find few souvenirs, just good food and good beer served up in a thoroughly German environment.

Schlenkerla's beer lineup includes three smoked beers. Year around they serve the regular rauchbier that is based on the Märzen style with an original specific gravity (OG) of 1.054 (13.5 °P) and 30 IBUs. Darkened by a small addition of roast malt, this flagship beer is deep amber to brown (28–30 SRM) with a cream-colored head. It presents a complex malty aroma with a clear smoked note and a matching flavor profile. A lingering malt and smoke note in the aftertaste invites further consumption, and the appealing smoke flavor remains clearly evident through a pint or even two. This is a beer that delivers on the promise of smoke flavor in both quality and quantity.

As a counterpoint to the Märzen, the other full-time beer at Schlenkerla is a weizen in which the barley malt is smoked but the wheat malt is not. The original gravity of this beer is nearly the same at 1.053 (13.2 °P), but it has a lower bitterness of just 17 or 18 IBUs. This entry has good smoke flavor and aroma upon first tasting. But the smoke tends to quickly submerge in the banana and clove weizen flavors that appropriately dominate a beer in this style.

Fall is bock time in Bamberg, and nearly all the local breweries hold a "Bock Anstich" or tapping day during October or early November to launch their own version of this popular seasonal specialty. Schlenkerla rolls out their Ur-Bock on the first Thursday in October, although we found that it was still available during our November visit. Bottles have also been imported into the United States in recent years.

The Schlenkerla Ur-Bock is quite dark—nearly black—with faint red highlights and is generally served with a good inch of foamy head. Made solely from Schlenkerla's smoked malt to an original gravity of 1.071 (17.5 °P), this beer gives an assertive smoke character even when one has already had smoked beer earlier in the day. Forty IBUs of bitterness create a clean balance without being aggressively bitter and result in a beer that is fully malty but never sweet.

In addition to these smoked products, Schlenkerla makes a Helles bier on a seasonal basis without smoked malt. We did not taste this beer, but local beer drinkers praised it as wonderful—although some claimed that they could taste just a touch of smoke left over from the brewery's regular products.

In recent years, the Schlenkerla beers have been imported to the United States and distributed to major markets. The year-round Märzen appears regularly, and the Ur-Bock arrived in 1999 and may be seen again in coming years.

The smaller Spezial brewery actually makes a broader range of beers, perhaps to provide extra variety for the regulars at their gasthaus where the vast majority of their beer is sold. The smoked lagers actually come in three varieties, a lager—what we would call a dunkel—at 1.048 SG (12 °P), a Märzen at 1.054 SG (13.5 °P), and the bock that weighs in at 1.069 SG (17 °P). Like Schlenkerla, they also make a weizen that, we were told, contains a "small amount" of smoked malt and also a seasonal beer without smoke character.

Visitors who make the mistake of visiting Schlenkerla before coming to Spezial may find the smoke flavor of these subtly tinted beers somewhat difficult to discern. But visitors who come with a clean, fresh palate find the smokiness both evident and delightful. The amber-colored lager presents an aroma with a firm smoke flavor and honeyish malt notes. In the palate, the smoke blends with the overall malt character of the beer to deliver a wonderful complexity with fleeting wood-smoke notes. The subtle bitterness provides a gentle balance in a light-bodied beer that seems perfect from start to finish.

Although Spezial's flagship märzen is more lightly smoked than that of its counterpart at Schlenkerla, it still offers a pronounced smoke flavor in a beer that is amber in color and medium bodied. The finish is crisp with little lingering sweetness, allowing the smoke to come back again and again as you drink.

The bock presents a subtle smoke character as part of an overall complexity that includes licorice and chocolate notes. This beer presents a good sweet note, which although far from cloying, is more sweet than most Bamberg bocks.

Those who visit Spezial in the spring or fall can sample the unsmoked *ungespundetes* lager—an unfiltered, lightly carbonated specialty also known as keller ("cellar") beer and best explained as the lager world's answer to cask-conditioned ale.

Our notes do not indicate that we drank the Spezial weizen—although surely we must have. Sometimes the best intentions at note-taking do get lost among the many distractions of pub-based beer tasting.

Other Bamberg-Style Rauch Beers

Although the two Bamberg-based brewers who still make their own smoked malt serve as the prototypes of the rauchbier art, other brewers in the area make smoked beers that are generally in the same style. During our visits to the area, we tracked down a number of notable examples.

Just five minute's drive east from Bamberg, one finds the small town of Memmelsdorf and a sparkling gasthaus called Drei Kronen. Here two great Bamberg brewing traditions come together in a single beer called Stöffla. This light brown beer is made generally in the style of a dunkel lager but with smoked malt. In addition, it is served unfiltered and keg-conditioned, thus making it a "keller" or "cellar" beer.

Stöffla presents a pleasant smoky flavor with a solid bitter finish that leaves little malt to linger in the aftertaste. Although the smoke is apparent when you first taste this beer, the palate quickly adapts, and by the time you have finished the first quarter liter, you really don't taste smoke anymore—just the barest hint in the palate and an occasional whisper in the aftertaste. Despite the subtle smokiness, this beer's recipe includes nearly 40 percent Weyermann rauch malt.

Drei Kronen proprietor Hans-Ludwig Straub learned English from American friends as a youth and welcomes English-speaking guests. Because of the demands of running a hotel and restaurant as well as a brewery, Straub's 10-hectoliter (8.5-barrel) brew house may get used only a few dozen times a year. Still, the combination of his beers with the delightful foods—which sometimes include sauces made from the beers—makes Drei Kronen a "must see" for visitors to the Bamberg area.

In marked contrast to Drei Kronen, the Barnikel Brewery south of Bamberg in the tiny village of Herrnsdorf offers a rural, rustic retreat from German formality. Surrounded by farms, the Barnikel Brewery resides in what was surely a barn in former times, and one can still see cows at milking in a neighboring building. The pub here is simple: one large square room with bare-wood floors and simple furnishings heated by a wood stove whose chimney pipe snakes precariously over one end of the *stammtisch*—or regulars' table.

All of the brewery's beers come in *Bügelflasche* (flip-top bottles), and the line-up includes dunkel, helles, weizen, and rauch. This rauchbier is 4.3 percent alcohol by weight (5.4 percent by volume) and displays a good bit of bready sweetness and some buttery notes in addition to a pleasant rauch flavor that remains apparent all the way to the bottom of the bottle. The eccentric menu includes things like ham, banana, and cheese pizza as well as traditional

Ray Daniels interviewing the braumeister of Brauerei Fischer.

schnitzels and wursts and a favorite Bamberg fish meal called Pfeffer Karpfen. (The German carp is quite different from the American version and is widely enjoyed here.)

Not far from Barnikel, we tracked down the enjoyable Brauerei (Brewery) Fischer in Greuth—a village so small that each house has its own two-digit number and streets go unnamed. We happened to arrive on a Friday—one of just two days when food is served in the cozy Fischer gasthaus. (Sunday is the other.) Here the rauchbier was deep amber to light brown in color with a pleasantly assertive smokiness and a nice balance complemented by a light body that made it easy to drink.

The current proprietor received his brewer's *Meisterbrief*—a sort of certification for crafts and trades—in 1990, but recalled that even his grandfather made rauchbier in the Fischer brewery. The current rauchbier recipe includes 50 percent smoked malt—although in this case it comes from a small maltster in the town of Erlangen.

One final Bamberg-style rauchbier is a feature of the Hummel Brewery in Merkendorf to the north of Bamberg. This beer, called "Räucherla" conforms to the classic definition of the style with a Märzenlike amber color and a distinct although not assertive smoke flavor. As with most well-made Märzens, it was pleasantly balanced with bitterness, but left a distinctively malty aftertaste.

In addition to these locally enjoyed rauch beers, we should make mention here of two other smoke-flavored beers that are sometimes distributed in the United States.

The first of these is Rauchenfels Steinbeer, a unique specialty product that immerses hot rocks (or "steins") in the wort during brewing. This light amber lager gives a smoky caramel aroma with a hint of burnt sugar. The palate reveals a pleasant malt sweetness with a distinct toasted note in mid-palate that evolves to a crisp finish. The pleasant wood smokiness is evident throughout and lingers in the finish.

Although heating rocks on a wood fire doesn't seem like a logical way to transfer smoked flavor to a beer, you can't deny the presence of smoke in this product. Thus, during the planning stages for this book, we intended to present "hot-rock brewing" as an alternative method for producing smoked flavor. Still, one regular maker of stone beers, Boscos brewpub owner and head brewer Chuck Skypeck, warned us that he had never been able to generate smoked flavor in a beer with this technique, even though he has been practicing it regularly on both home and commercial scales for more than ten years. While in Bamberg, we inquired about this and discovered that the German stein beer, Rauchenfels, is indeed made from a grist that includes smoked malt. Thus the beer earns a place in the line-up of German smoked beers, but stone brewing loses out as an alternative production technique because we can find no evidence that this technique alone is capable of producing smoke flavor.

Another beer that longtime fans of Bamberg smoked beers will be curious about is a product marketed in the United States as Kaiserdom Rauchbier. This smoked Märzen was distributed widely in the United States during the late 1980s and early 1990s and still sees some limited distribution today. This beer comes from the Kaiserdom Brewery on the northwest edge of Bamberg, but it is not distributed in Germany. This brewery—one of Bamberg's largest—makes a wide range of products for export in addition to some popular and creative beers for the German market. Although they do not sell this rauchbier in Germany, they have begun to use smoked malt in another beer recently—and its story brings us to the next category of smoked-malt beers, a category that might be called "stealth smoke."

The German Secret: Subtle Smoke Gives Complexity

In addition to beers that exhibit smoke as a primary flavor component, we found several that took a very different approach. Here brewers use rauch malt in small proportions to create beers in which smoke merely contributes to malt complexity without asserting itself as a readily discernible flavor component.

One of the recent innovations from the Kaiserdom Brewery is a product called Meranier Schwarzbier—a black lager spiced with a pinch of Weyermann smoked malt. Black and nearly opaque, this beer reflects the renewed interest in dark beers by German consumers. It displays mild roast and malt notes in the aroma, with perhaps just the barest hint of smoke. Indeed those who are unaware of the smoked-malt content would be unable to discern the faint smoked note of this beer.

We sampled the Meranier beer with brewery proprietors Georg and Magrit Wörner at their beautiful and historic gasthaus called *Rathausschänke*, which stands on the east side of the landmark bridge leading to Bamberg's beautifully restored *Rathaus* (town hall). Over a refreshingly unique lunch, we sorted out the confusion about the use of smoked malt in the beer. Some brewery employees had told us that the beer did not contain smoked malt, perhaps thinking that we would object to it. Nonetheless, Herr Wörner assured us of its presence in the beer. Of course our palates—blasted with smoke from many days of drinking rauchbier at that point, were unable to detect it at the time.

The subtle use of smoked malt in Kaiserdom's Meranier Schwarzbier sets the stage for other beers in which smoke is a secondary or tertiary flavor component.

One of the first beers Ray was introduced to in Franconia was served up in Würgau—the Hartmann Brewery's Felsentrunk. This Pilsener–like beer was deep gold to light amber with the incredible foam head typical of German lagers. It was described as having "*einem Hauch von rauch*"—a breath or hint of smoke. True enough, upon tasting, it was medium bodied and quite crisp with just a touch of identifiable smoke. Despite the Pilsenerlike balance, it left a nice lingering malt character in the aftertaste where the smoke hit just a bit.

Another example of this strategy was found in the small town of Hirschaid just a ten-minute train ride south of Bamberg. Here Brauerei Kraus makes a Festbier at 4.4 percent alcohol by weight (5.5 percent by volume) that displays just a hint of smoke. Listed as *Hirschentrunk* (deer draught?) on the menu, this beer displayed a good bit of hop character in both the palate and the finish. Here too, smoked malt played a minor but still important role in creating the overall flavor of a very enjoyable beer.

The final example of this approach comes from Kaiser Bräu, in Neuhaus, a small town about 25 miles east of Bamberg. This unique dunkel beer (color, 17 SRM), called Echt Veldensteiner Landbier, is named after a well-known castle in the area. Brewed to an original gravity of 1.049 SG (12.3 °P), the grist includes Weyermann rauch malt for 10 percent of the total, with Vienna accounting for the majority. (We include a recipe based on this beer later in the book.) It is modestly bittered at 16 IBUs and reveals just a subtle hint of smokiness in the palate.

The American Approach to Smoke—Commercially Produced Smoked Beers in the United States

In the past decade, the interest in smoked beer has increased owing to several factors including the growing number of brewpubs and the addition of smoke-flavored beer as its own style in the Great American Beer Festival. Prior to these events, smoked beers in the United States were primarily made by homebrewers and a very few of the new craft breweries.

For commercial breweries, the smoked-beer category, or style, was revived in the United States in 1990 when the Great American Beer Festival expanded the number of categories for judging and included rauch as a separate style. Until that time, only a few U.S. breweries were dabbling with the addition of smoke flavor in beer. London-based beer writer Michael Jackson had enthusiastically described one of the beers—Geoff's own Alaskan Smoked Porter—in several of his reviews and essays (Jackson, 1990, p. 6). That favorable review and the addition of rauch as a style of its own was duly noted by the fledgling craft beer industry, and the number of smoked commercial beers began to grow.

Also in the 1990s, the number of pub breweries in the United States increased dramatically. The new brewpubs were seeking to establish unique identities to entice customers to their establishments. Brewers at the pubs began increasing the range of styles offered at their pubs. In addition, because of the growth of the number of establishments, many more brewers were employed. Brewpub brewers were often given more freedom than those at the larger commercial breweries to "create" house brews for the pub. Smoked beers were especially intriguing to those brewers looking to pair beer and food, as many of the pub situations began to offer expanded menus to their guests.

The new brewers experimented with various methods of adding smoke to their brews. Commercially available smoked malt is limited. In the United States, it is mainly available from only two suppliers, both of whom are in Europe. As we have described, Bairds of Scotland produces a peat-smoked malt, and Weyermann of Germany produces a beechwood-smoked malt. Unlike the older institutional brewers, pub brewers generally came from a strong homebrew background. This led them to be more experimental, trying recipes using everything from liquid smoke to smoking their own malt on a barbecue grill. Still others tried using commercial smokehouses in their locale for smoking their malt, and a few used their pub roasters. As interest in the smoked-beer style grew and refinements from brewers and malt suppliers alike helped to produce more consistent smoke-flavored beers, the smoke enthusiast began talking about finding these unique brews from one end of the United States to the other.

One can now find brewers in as far-flung states as Alaska, Hawaii, and Vermont; all are producing smoked beers for their local region. Generally offered only seasonally, these beers are most often found in brewpubs. Brewers tend to either use commercially smoked malt from one of the two suppliers, or they smoke their own and use a variety of woods. (Only Rogue Brewing mixes Weyermann smoked malt with his own alderwood-

Kiawe Wood

Kiawe wood is a hardwood similar to hickory or mesquite. It is indigenous to the Hawaiian Islands and produces a smoked malt that has fruity and/or sweet overtones, while maintaining robust smoky properties.

smoked malt.) Apple, alder, hickory, Hawaiian kiawe, maple, mesquite, and mountain mahogany are some of the woods used. Unlike the smoked-beer style in Bamberg, which has many years of tradition dictating the use of beechwood, U.S. smoked beers are in the experimental stages and are not bound by tradition. Some breweries have used woods indigenous to their locations such as Alaskan Brewing Company's use of alderwood chips or Brew Moon's use of kiawe wood in Hawaii. Some use a blend of various woods to create a unique smoke flavor such as Vermont Brewing Company's combination of apple, maple, and hickory.

We have compiled a list of commercially available smoked beers in the United States. We include a cross section of them here.

Smoked Beers Using Commercially Smoked Malt

DeGroen's Rauchbock: Theo DeGroen, Baltimore Brewing Company, 104 Albemarle Street, Baltimore, Maryland 21212; telephone (410) 887-5000. Available March–April. Using 20% Weyermann's beechwood-smoked malt, this rauchbock is a multiple-award winner including a gold medal at the 1999 Great American Beer Festival.

Notes: Blonde to orange head, this crisp bock is nicely balanced with a pleasant smoke backing and maltiness. The aroma has a nutty character complementing the beechwood smoke. The beer has a slight brown hue hinting of the rich malty flavor that is semisweet and complex yet well balanced with a clean hop bitterness. The smoke flavor is mellow but obvious.

OG: 1.0633 (15.5 °P)
ABV: 6.7%
IBUs: 20
SRM: 15
Hop variety: Hallertau Hersbrucker, Nuggets
Malt: two-row pale, Munich, Caramunich, and Weyermann rauch
Date first brewed commercially: 1997

Arcadia London Porter: George Murphy, Arcadia Brewing Company, 103 West Michigan Avenue, Battle Creek, Michigan 49017; telephone (616) 963-9520. Available November–January; sold in bottles throughout Michigan and Chicago. This bottle-conditioned robust porter is brewed each year in August for release during the holiday season and derives its smoke flavor from Weyermann's beechwood-smoked malt.

Notes: This dark and rich-looking beer visually prepares you for the chocolate malt aroma that greets you. The subdued beechwood smoke blends well with the malt and lets the low but perceivable hop aromas come through. There is a hint of molasses that adds to this complex bouquet. The flavor of smoke is balanced with fruity and spicy notes. There is alcoholic warmth to this beer. The finish is long and smooth.

OG: 1.082 (19.8 °P)
ABV: 7%
IBUs: 42
SRM: 118
Hop variety: Fuggles, Goldings
Malt: British—two-row pale, crystal, chocolate, and black
Belgian—Munich and Dark Special B
German—Weyermann beechwood rauch
Date first brewed commercially: 1997

Smokin' Ale: Steve Schmidt, Empire Brewing Company of Syracuse, Armory Square, 120 Walton Street, Syracuse, New York 13202; telephone (315) 475-4409. Available during the fall. Empire Brewing has three pubs in Buffalo, Rochester, and Syracuse, New York. Their Smokin' Ale is brewed in Syracuse but served at all three pubs. The smoke flavor comes from Weyermann malt.

Notes: This beer is brilliantly clear and golden with orange highlights. The aroma is clearly of smoke with slight caramel and tangy phenolic notes to it. Mild medium body with a tad of sweetness, ending with a light hop finish. A refreshing brew!

OG: 1.059 (14.5 °P)
ABV: 5.6%
IBUs: 25
SRM: 7.8
Hop variety: Hallertau Hersbrucker, Perle
Malt: All German including Weyermann beechwood rauch
Date first brewed commercially: 1996

Rich's Rauch Bier: Rich Becker, J.T. Whitney's Pub and Brewery, 674 South Whitney Way, Madison, Wisconsin 53711; telephone (608)-274-1776. Available during the summer and fall. This award-winning Märzen uses Weyermann's beechwood-smoked malt and was inspired by the German brewmaster's family heritage.

Notes: A light amber lager with a beautiful head of foam. The foam remains in the glass, releasing a clean but subtle maplelike smoky aroma. Nice malt flavor, subdued hops with a medium body and a lingering slightly sweet finish.

OG: 1.0547 (13.5 °P)
ABV: 5.7%
IBUs: 28
SRM: 70–80
Hop variety: Perle, Hallertau, and Tettnang
Malt: two-row pale, Munich, crystal, chocolate, and Weyermann rauch
Date first brewed commercially: 1996

Stone Smoked Porter: Steve Wagner, Stone Brewing Company, 155 Mata Way, # 104, San Marcos, California 92069; telephone (760) 471-4999. Available in California and Arizona.

Notes: This beer is almost opaque with ruby highlights. The malty sweet aroma is complex with an elusive mint–like character and an earthy note that probably comes from the peat-smoked malt. Smoke aroma and flavor is subdued. Caramel flavor cut with roasted and chocolate notes provides a rich, dry finish to this beer.

OG: 1.0655 (16 °P)
ABV: 5.8%
IBUs: 47
SRM: 103
Hop variety: Nugget, Mt. Hood
Malt: two-row pale, crystal, chocolate, and Hugh Baird Light (4–6 ppm phenolic content) peat-smoked malt
Date first brewed commercially: 1996

Smoked Beers Using Self-Smoked Malt

Alaskan Smoked Porter: Geoff Larson, Alaskan Brewing Company, 5429 Shaune Drive, Juneau, Alaska 99801; telephone (907) 780-5966. Available December–February. A pioneer of smoked beers in North America, this beer has won numerous awards and is available on draft and in bottles. It is vintage dated. The brewers use alder chips to smoke the malt in a commercial smokehouse (Taku Smokeries) located in Juneau. Alder is commonly found in Alaska and has been used historically to preserve many traditional foods in the area.

Notes: A dark, bold, complex beer with a pronounced smoky flavor. The woody smoke aroma, while assertive, still allows the late-addition hops and the chocolate characters to come through in the aroma. The malty, chocolaty body backs up a balanced yet assertively hopped beer. This beer ages well with the flavor developing nicely over time. In older vintages, dried fruit characters are acquired, which with the subsiding bitterness create a sweeter aftertaste. With age, the smoke characters tend to recede, and so, while still recognizable, the smoke becomes more of an accent to the sherrylike overtones.

OG: 1.065 (15.9 °P)
ABV: 6.1%
IBUs: 45
SRM: 92
Hop variety: Chinook and Willamette
Malt: two-row pale, Munich, two types of caramel, chocolate, and black patent
Date first brewed commercially: 1988

Hickory Switch Smoked Amber Ale: Lawrence Miller, Otter Creek Brewing, 85 Exchange Street, Middlebury, Vermont 05753; telephone (800) 473-0727. Available September–November. Lawrence Miller uses hickory to smoke a portion of their malt bill for this beer. The brewery smokes the malt that they use in a specially built smokehouse.

Notes: This amber ale has a beautiful creamy head that exhibits a slight orange hue. The aroma is

balanced in that hickory and malt both are clearly evident in the aroma. The smoke aroma and flavor are moderate, letting the rest of the beer express itself. This is a medium-bodied beer, with vinous notes and smoky dryness balancing the sweet malts. Available in bottles and draft.

OG: *1.047 (11.7 °P)*
ABV: 4.5%
IBUs: 18
SRM: n/a
Hop variety: Chinook, Hallertau, Tettnang, Cascade, and Willamette
Malt: two-row pale, Munich, caramel 60, Carapils, chocolate
Date first brewed commercially: 1991

Kiawe Smoked Lager: Scott Hutchinson, Brewmoon Restaurant and Microbrewery, 115 Stuart Street, City Place, Boston, Massachusetts 02116; telephone (781) 707-2220. Available winter and spring months. Munich malt is cold smoked with kiawe chips and apple wood. The malt is spread out on sheet pans, misted with water, and then placed in a smoker. The Brewmoon operates five brewpubs: three in Massachusetts, one in Pennsylvania, and one in Hawaii. Brewmoon brewers use the smoked malt for brewing three different styles of beer, at all five locations. This schwarzbier is their favorite.

OG: 1.051 (12.8 °P)
ABV: 5.2%
IBUs: 45
SRM: 20
Hop variety: Hallertau, m.f. and Vanguard
Malt: two-row pale lager malt, Carafa, chocolate malt, wheat, crystal, Munich 10 and 26, and malt smoked with kiawe and
apple woods
Date first brewed commercially: 1999

Sweetwater Chipotle Porter: Nick Funnell, Sweetwaer Tavern & Brewery, 3066 Gatehouse Plaza, Fall Church, Virginia 22042; telephone (703) 449-1100. Sweetwater has two pubs with a southwestern theme, the second pub is located in Centreville, VA. Sweetwater offers their Chipotle Porter seasonally, on draft only. The Chipotle Porter is brewed with chipotle chilis. Chipotle chilis are actually jalapeño peppers dried over a direct fire. This process smokes the peppers during the drying. The brewers hand-smoke their pale malt in their restaurant smoker using mesquite chips. This beer has been offered both filtered and unfiltered, and according to Nick Funnell the filtered version has been the more popular of the two.

Notes: Chocolate richness giving way to a smoky finish, with not-too-hot echoes of smoked jalapeño heat that begins soft and heats the mouth after the malt fades to the background. The pepper spiciness adds a very interesting dimension to this beer without being distracting at all. The complex smoke character in this beer is from two sources which is best described as both earthy (from the smoked jalapeños) and peaty (from the mesquite).

OG: 1.0526 (13°P)
ABW: 5.5%
IBUs: 28
SRM: n/a
Hop variety: Cluster, Willamette, plus dried chipotle chilies
Malt: English pale, crystal, DeWulf Cosyus Special Roast, choclate, black, and mesquite smoked pale malt.
Date first brewed commercially: April 1998

Vermont Smoked Porter: Greg Noonan, Vermont Pub and Brewery, 144 College Street, Burlington, Vermont 05401; telephone (802) 865-0500. Available at the pub and in growlers to go all year long. After experimenting with several different woods, they have settled on using a blend of apple, maple, and hickory.

Notes: This complex and opaque porter has a fine creamy head. The aroma that is released from the foam has a beautiful rich smoke character. While assertive, the aroma lets the beer express the flavors that you would expect in a porter, backed with the body to balance the hopping and the smoke. There is no mistaking that this is a smoked beer, but the flavor is mellow and complex. The aftertaste is exquisite as the characters of the smoke linger on the palate. Greg Noonan explains that the smoke of apple wood is what gives the malt a rich, smooth smoke base. However, he also uses a small amount of hickory and maple wood in smoking the malt. Greg says the hickory adds a touch of smoky phenolic highlights to the beer, and the maple adds a bit of a smoky bite to this outstanding product.

OG: 1.060 (14.7 °P)
ABV: 5.8%
IBUs: 45
SRM: 27
Hop variety: Perle
Malt: pale, wheat, Carapils, crystal, chocolate, and malt smoked with maple, hickory, and apple woods
Date first brewed commercially: 1989

Smoked Beers Using Both! Commercially Smoked Malt and Self-Smoked Malt

Rogue Smoke: John Maier, Rogue Brewing Company, 2320 OSU Drive, Newport, Oregon 97369; telephone (541) 867-3660. Available year-round in 7-ounce bottles and draft.

Notes: This multiple-award-winning beer uses Weyermann beechwood-smoked pale malt and in-house alderwood-smoked Munich malt. It was first released under the name Welcommen—a roguish Americanization of the German word for welcome, Wilkommen. Rouge Smoke is a deep amber-hued lager with a white lacey head that lingers. This beer has a rich smoky flavor along with Maier's signature hop bite, followed by a crisp dry finish. The caramel flavors and body balance the bitterness and smokiness. The long, rich, and lingering aftertaste has made this beer a classic in the category. There is no question that the smoke aroma is reminiscent of the beers of Bamberg—and for good reason too, as the majority of the malt bill used in this beer is Weyermann rauch malt from Bamberg. However, John Maier adds a bit of the "Northwest" with some alderwood-smoked malt. John says this adds a richness that complements the dry smoke flavors of the beechwood smoke. The alderwood malt has more smoke intensity than the Weyermann malt; therefore it accounts for a fraction of the malt bill.

OG: 1.0568 (14 °P)
ABV: 5.6%
IBUs: 48
SRM: 30
Hop variety: Perle, Saaz
Malt: two-row pale, Weyermann beechwood-smoked pale, alderwood-smoked Munich, crystal
Date first brewed commercially: 1990

Other Smoke-Flavored Beers

In the first two sections of this chapter, we have covered the broad range of smoked beers that flourish today in Franconia and across the United States. To conclude this subject and include the full scope of the smoke and malt minglings, we present the odds and ends as it were—a selection of beers and styles that may be rare, but still deserve mention.

Let us begin by picking up on the peat-smoked malt theme that we saw in America. Although the U.S. trend may be based on the notion that Scottish beers may have once contained peat-smoked malt, there is a European entry that is odder still. The beer is called Adelscott—a French-brewed specialty with an assertive, but generally pleasant peat-smoked flavor.

At one time, this product was imported to the United States, but we have not seen it in some time, and our requests for information—sent to the brewery in France—have not generated any reply. Nonetheless, the product represents the European side of the "whiskey malt" branch of the smoked-beer family. Ray remembers Adelscott as a fully amber-colored beer with modest bitterness. Indeed, Michael Jackson tells us that the beer was made to an original gravity of 1.065 (16 °P) and contained only 20 to 22 IBUs.

This listing nearly exhausts our harvest of European beers made with smoked flavor. We have heard stories of one or two others, but few details have emerged. Dutch brewers told us of a smoked bock beer found in the eastern part of Holland called "De Hemel" or "The Heaven." Like many of the German smoked-malt entries, it is made with Weyermann malt and offered seasonally starting in early October. Sadly, our travels did not allow us to taste this beer.

Britain seems nearly devoid of wood-smoked beers. Only one or two rumors of their existence reached our ears—and these lacked sufficient detail for follow-up.

Although we have focused our investigations on England, continental Europe, and the United States, these are not the only areas where one can find smoke-flavored beers. Japan has had a number of small breweries open in the last decade, and a few of them offer beer with smoke flavor, some of which are already winning awards. Breweries either use commercially available rauch malt or they make their own. Either approach can produce wonderful beers. In the next chapter we describe how brewers can make their own malt so that a regional smoke flavor can be expressed in the beer that is made with it.

CHAPTER 4

The Chemistry of Smoke

Okay, here it is, the chapter you've been dreading—or maybe hoping for. The one with the long chemical names that you will never remember, and the little stick-figure drawings (actually, we have remarkably few of either). So fear not. Neither of us finds glee in tedious chemistry. If you wish, you can skip this chapter entirely and still make great smoked beers. But we have included it for a reason. Wood smoking, like brewing, is a chemically complex process. If you really want to make good smoke-flavored beers, and especially if you want to smoke your own malts successfully, then you truly should have a basic grasp of what is going on when you use fire to transfer the character of wood smoke from a collection of chips and logs to a pile of malt.

Until recently, smoke has been pervasive and even ubiquitous in the human environment. For many millennia, fire was used to warm homes, cook foods, and light the way. But every fire is not the same. Even in our modern world, which is nearly free of smelly smokes, most people can tell the difference between a fire that is fueled by mesquite and one that is fed by hickory.

It should come as no surprise then that the chemistry of smoke is directly tied to the fuel that is used. Whether you burn fossil fuels (petroleum, natural gas, or coal) or some other organic flammable (straw, wood, peat, camel dung, or ferns, for example), you will get chemically similar end products. Similar, but not exactly the same. As with our good friend the hop, it turns out that the smallest trace fractions of chemical differences in the source materials create palpable variations in the flavor characteristics that they impart.

And it doesn't stop there. If the process of burning is accomplished with 100 percent efficiency—in the presence of sufficient oxygen—the fuel's hydrocarbons are reduced to nothing more than carbon dioxide, water, and heat without any smoke. Although heat is what humans have typically sought from fire, the fact that we live in an imperfect world means that combustion is never ideal. Thus fire generally creates some smoke. The amount and character of smoke from a fire are influenced by a range of conditions that we explore in this chapter.

In this chapter, our discussion is confined to those flavor properties imparted to malt by smoke itself. We leave to others a discussion of those reactions that commonly occur when green or wet malt is exposed to heat from *any* source. This broader subject includes Maillard reactions, which produce many of the color and flavor compounds in malt, caramelization of sugars, and toasting or charring of malt constituents. All of these processes may contribute to the flavors of your smoked malt, and you are nearly certain to encounter them each time you thrust a damp pile of malt into a smoky chamber. However, unlike the flavors that come from smoke, these other reactions are mediated by heat alone and, as a result, are well documented in texts that cover malt and malting.

We begin our discussion of smoke by looking at the composition of the source material, wood. From there we consider the dynamics of fire itself. Then the real fun begins when we put the two together and look at the results. To bring things back to the brewer's perspective, we next move our focus to the malt itself to see how the flavor of smoke is apprehended and incorporated. Finally, we make a trip to the dark side of smoke and talk about how you can prevent the creation of unhealthy substances when you make smoked malt.

Wood

Botanically, trees fall into two different categories—hardwoods and softwoods. Hardwoods produce woody seeds with two halves, usually exhibit broad leaves, and are typically deciduous. Softwoods produce seed cones and have needle-like leaves that remain green year round (also known as evergreens).

For smoking purposes, softwoods can be dismissed because they contain up to 5 percent of a class of compounds called terpenes. This class includes turpentine and resins that confer a distinct and undesirable flavor to the smoke from these woods. Some hardwoods, such as ironwood and teak, have especially high wax and resin contents and also do not produce good-tasting smoke. Fortunately, however, most other hardwoods lack these problems and can be used to produce attractively flavored smoked products.

Wood is made up primarily of natural polymers. Although the word *polymer* is familiar to everyone these days, because we use it a lot, it is valuable to recall its scientific meaning. Simply stated, a polymer is a large molecule or chemical structure made up many *identical* building blocks linked end to end or side to side. A long row of identical town homes would be one model. A lengthy string of sausages might be another.

Wood consists primarily of three polymers: Cellulose, hemicellulose, and lignin. In hardwoods, cellulose makes up 40 to 45 percent of wood's dry weight; hemicellulose accounts for 20 to 35 percent; and lignin generally makes up 18 to 38 percent. One source we found simplifies this "wood recipe" as "about ½ cellulose, ¼ hemicellulose, and ¼ lignin"—a crude approximation perhaps, but easy to remember.

Cellulose consists of long chains of glucose (Maga, 1988, p. 2). In that respect, it is very similar to the barley starch from which we make beer. Both are built from glucose; both occur in long unbranched chains. Of course starch also forms branched molecules in its more common form. In addition, we know that the bond that links the glucose molecules of cellulose is different (1-4β) from that found in straight starch (1-4α).

Like cellulose, hemicellulose is also made up of sugars, but the resemblance stops there. Hemicellulose contains various five- and six-carbon sugars, although the pentose xylose is always present in the largest amount. In contrast to cellulose, which is crystalline and strong, hemicellulose has a random, amorphous structure with little strength.

Lignin is a high-molecular-weight, randomly cross-linked polymer. It is derived primarily from three aromatic alcohols, *p*-coumaryl, coniferyl, and sinapyl (Simonelt et al., 1993). The proportions of these constituents vary considerably among the major plant classes. Thus, lignins of hardwoods are enriched in products from sinapyl alcohol, softwoods instead have a high proportion of products from coniferyl alcohol with a minor component from sinapyl alcohol, and grasses have mainly products from *p*-coumaryl alcohol (Simonelt et al., 1993). As we show, these differences have a lot to do with the flavor character of smoke.

Beyond the three primary polymers, the other components of wood include extractives (less than 5 percent) and ash (less than 1 percent). The extractives include tannins, starches, resins, oils, alkaloids, and other miscellaneous components. Ash consists of inorganic substances, for example, calcium, potassium, and iron.

Generally, the extractives tend to change or diminish significantly with the seasoning of wood. Thus it is interesting that the aging of wood is a traditional practice in Bamberg. And although the explanation is mainly for reasons of decreasing the moisture content in wood, this aging also changes the extractives that influence the organoleptic properties of the smoke produced. This may be a significant effect, as bark and its inner lining have a lot of the extractives in both hardwoods and softwoods.

Extractives

As the name implies, extractives are the soluble compounds that exist in wood and bark. We mean here both water and organic-solvent miscible. Many of these compounds are volatile and will leave the bark via evaporation. Seasoning or aging of wood gives enough time for this process to occur. So the use of the term "wood drying" is not quite accurate as you can remoisten the wood after aging, but you will not get any of the extractives back.

From this description, it is easy to see that wood consists primarily of sugars that have been bound into complex polymeric structures. Living things from yeasts to the human body burn sugars and their complex cousins, carbohydrates, as a source of energy. It should come as no surprise then that sugar-rich wood makes an excellent fuel when "burning" takes place in the literal sense in a classic red-flame fire.

Fire

Like some other things that seem so simple on the surface (beer and relationships come to mind), a wood fire is devilishly complex underneath. Before we can explore the chemical entities that give smoked malt its flavor, we have to begin to understand what happens when wood burns. But have no fear: fire itself is interesting, and we promise to keep the presentation nice and simple.

Let's start with this fact: Wood itself does not burn. Combustion, or fire, is a rapid oxidation reaction that liberates heat and light. In order to occur, fire must have all three sides of the classic "fire triangle," namely fuel, heat, and oxygen. Since wood is a solid substance, oxygen can not mix with the "fuel" and therefore combustion of a wood + oxygen mixture is not possible.

What actually happens when wood burns is a two-step process. In step one, wood is heated and undergoes a thermal degradation. This occurs in the relative absence of oxygen and is known as pyrolysis.

The pyrolysis of wood results in two groups of products—volatiles and char. As the name implies, the volatiles make up a gaseous substance that includes many different chemical species such as simple gases like carbon monoxide, carbon dioxide, and hydrogen as well as some hydrocarbons and other small organic compounds such as aldehydes, acids, ketones, and alcohols. The char consists largely of carbon.

After pyrolysis, the second step in the production of fire from wood can take place. When the volatile gases produced by pyrolysis mix with oxygen from the air in the presence of adequate heat, they ignite and burn. Voilà! We have fire.

Combustion is an exothermic reaction—that is, it generates heat. A portion of this heat causes pyrolysis of the surrounding raw wood, liberating more flammable volatiles and sustaining the flames. Thus fire, once started, is a self-sustaining process limited only by the availability of fuel and oxygen.

Okay, so that covers the "flaming" part of fire. But there is more.

For starters, pyrolysis can occur when there isn't enough heat or oxygen present to ignite the volatiles. This is called smoldering. Although smoldering generates a lot of smoke, the character of the smoke will be different from that produced by a flaming fire. Why? Because the flames that normally accompany a fire oxidize and break-down the volatile products of pyrolysis. Without flames, the volatiles escape unchanged. Now we can't say for sure just exactly what the chemical differences are, but we do know that some barbecue purists say that the smoke from smoldering wood should be avoided like the plague as it imparts a nasty creosote flavor.

The char that results from pyrolysis can also burn, although generally without the presence of a flame. This "glowing combustion" is what's seen when you burn wood down to coals. The coals are still "burning"—although with a hot red glow that may only occasionally be punctuated by brief wisps of flame. During this process, the burning char liberates heat as well as a thin blue smoke. Many connoisseurs of barbecue look to this smoke as the most desirable source of positive smoke flavors.

To summarize, wood doesn't burn. Instead, it pyrolyzes or decomposes when exposed to heat. Following pyrolysis we may see—individually or together—three different effects: A smoky smolder, a full-flame fire, or a glowing burn of the blackened char. To better understand these effects, let's move on to look in more detail at the chemistry of wood as it burns.

Burning Wood

As we have already mentioned, fire involves oxidation. In its perfect form, fire reduces complex carbon-based structures into simple molecules of carbon dioxide (CO_2). This end product—a carbon atom bound to two oxygen atoms—is carbon in its most oxidized form.

In general, the simpler the fuel, the more likely it is that all the carbon structures will be completely converted to CO_2. But as we have already seen, wood is a very complicated fuel that consists of large, complex molecules built from many different building blocks. As a result, much of the carbon-containing material in wood is not converted to CO_2 when burned. Instead, these materials produce a wide range of end-products that contribute to the characteristic smoke flavor imparted by the wood. In this section, we strive to better understand the formation and identity of the important flavor compounds that come from burning wood.

We must note, however, that we are now venturing into an area of imperfect knowledge. Although much is known about wood fires and even smoke, some critical insights remain hidden, especially when it comes to the various techniques by which one might smoke malt on a small scale. Having said that, let us begin with what we *do* know and move forward into the areas of uncertainty.

When it comes to the chemical basis of smoke, experts agree that cellulose is the body of smoke, although lignin is the soul. In more practical terms, this poetry means that most of what makes up the smoke comes from the closely related cellulose and hemicellulose, but it is the lignin combustion that accents the pleasurable smoky elements of it. We know that certain smoke compounds come from the cellulose part of wood whereas others clearly come from the lignin part. To a reasonable degree, we can even characterize the flavors imparted by these compounds.

Hemicellulose is the first of the three main polymers of wood to decompose upon heating. It generates compounds called furans along with aliphatic carboxylic acids (Maga, 1988, p. 29). The burning of this component of the wood contributes breadlike, sweet, and caramellike flavors and aromas.

Cellulose breaks down next, producing a broad range of compounds including aliphatic heterocyclic hydrocarbons, furans, lactones, carbonyls, alcohols, ketones, aldehydes, acid esters, a few phenols, and aromatics (Maga, 1988, p. 30). This component of the wood gives smoke much of the nutty, woody, sweet caramellike burnt

TABLE 1

Key Flavor Compounds from the Pyrolysis of Wood

From Cellulose Pyrolysis	From Lignin Pyrolysis
acetic acid—vinegar	phenolortho-, meta-, and para-cresols
formic acid	guaiacol—sweet, smoky, pungent*
maltol	4-methylguaiacol
methyl cyclopentenolone—brandy or caramel, smoked ham, cloves*	4-ethylguaiacol
ethylcyclopentenolone	4-propylguaiacol
dimethylcyclopentenolones	pyrocatechol—heavy, sweet, and
burnt*	
furfural	trimethylphenols
5-hydroxymethylfurfural	vanillin
	4-(2-propio)-vanillone
	4-(1-propio)-vanillone
	acetovanillone
	2,4,5-trimethylbenzaldehyde
	4-hydroxyacetophenone
	eugenol
	cis- and trans-isoeugenol
	2,6-dimethoxyphenol (syringol)
	4-methylsyringol
	4-ethylsyringol
	4-propylsyringol
	4-acetosyringol
	4-(2-propio)-syringol
	4-(1-propio)-syringol
	cis- and trans-4-(1-propenyl)-syringol
	4-(2-propenyl)-syringol
	syringaldehyde

*Guillen and Manzanos (1999).

characters. Table 1 shows the key flavor compounds that come from cellulose.

Cellulose and hemicellulose form mainly volatile products on heating because of the thermal breakdown of the sugar units; however, some char is also formed from these components (Shafizadeh, 1982, p. 749). Although the char is fairly simple chemically, being composed primarily of carbon, the volatile products are more complex. One source breaks the volatile fraction into three sections as follows (Shafizadeh, 1981, p. 107):

Gas fraction:	CO, CO_2, H_2, some hydrocarbons
Condensable fraction:	Low-molecular-weight organic compounds: aldehydes, acids, ketones, alcohols
Tar fraction:	Higher-molecular-weight sugar residues, furan derivatives, phenolic compounds, and airborne particles of tar and charred material that form the smoke

Although a raging fire may give off this full range of products, research has shown that the components of the volatile fraction may vary considerably when temperatures are lower.

Pyrolysis Reactions at Different Temperatures

Grant Ballard-Tremeer (1997) has analyzed the emissions of rural wood-burning cooking devices and has come up with the following pyrolytic products depending on the temperature range involved:

Below 300 °C	carbonyl, carboxyl, CO, and CO_2 mainly as a charred residue
Between 300 and 450 °C	a mixture of levoglucosan, anhydrides, and oligosaccharides largely as a "tar" fraction
Above 450 °C	a variety of carbonyl compounds such as acetaldehyde, glyoxal, and acrolein that evaporate easily
Above 500 °C	a mixture of all of these products

So, Ballard-Tremeer's data tell us a good bit about the body of smoke, which comes from cellulose and hemicellulose. Now what about the soul of smoke, the stuff that comes from lignin?

Lignin is the last of the three wood polymers to pyrolyze when heated and requires temperatures of about 400 °C to do so (Guillen and Ibargoitia, 1996). Because lignin's structure is not readily broken down to lower-molecular-weight fragments, the pyrolysis of lignin produces more char than volatiles—although the exact ratio between these two products is highly dependent upon burning conditions (Shafizadeh, 1981, p. 107; 1982, p. 749, 758).

The all-important phenolic compounds in smoke come primarily from thermal degradation of lignin (Guillen and Ibargoitia, 1998). Lignin's decomposition

Flavors of Chemical Groups Generated During Wood Combustion

A wide range of flavors is possible as a result of wood combustion. Here is a list of the main groups of compounds generated during wood combustion and the flavors associated with them (from Maga, 1988, pp. 76, 302–320):

Heterocyclic hydrocarbons: Nutty, woody, caramel, sweet cornlike, cereal, roasted.

Furans: Sweet, caramel, burnt, butterscotch, breadlike, grassy, balsamic.

Lactones: Burnt, bitter, sour, caramel, vanilla, sweet.

Carbonyls: Grassy, bitter, potatolike (diacetyl is a carbonyl).

Carboxylic acids: Sharp, acrid.

Alcohols: Spirituous, sweet, oily.

Ketones: Fruity, floral.

Aldehydes: Pungent, irritant, fruity.

Esters: Floral.

Phenols: Spicy, smoky, medicinal.

Pyrazines: Roasted nutlike, earthy, popcorn, burnt, roasted (in some cases butterscotch).

produces most of the phenols, phenolic esters of guaiacol and syringol, and their homologues, derivatives, and associated compounds. Vanillin, vanillic acid, and acetovanillone are also combustion products of lignin (Maga, 1988, p. 34). A list of the key flavor compounds produced by lignin is shown in Table 1.

There is also a set of eight pyrazine compounds that are of interest in smoking. Their appearance in wood does not coincide with any of the other organic chemical constituents (e.g., terpenes) or polymer structures (lignin, cellulose, and hemicellulose) that we have discussed so far. By all indications, they are species specific—for example, spruce species (e.g., Norway spruce, White spruce, and Sitka spruce) all have similar lignin and nitrogen content, but there seems to be no similarity when comparing the pyrazine compounds they contain. Still, these nitrogen-substituted aromatic rings have significant organoleptic properties that are believed to include roasted nutlike, earthy, popcorn, burnt, and roasted characters.

At this point, we have identified many key flavor compounds (Table 1) that come from smoke, and we are nearly done with the "theory" part of our discussion. But before we move on to see how what we've learned might direct the practice of smoking, we have one more essential stop to make. Here we'll visit the dark side of smoke.

The Dark Side

Throughout this book we have talked about smoke in a positive light on the basis of its historical significance, its role in food preservation, and of course its function as a pleasurable flavor enhancer. But like most things in this world, smoke is not perfect. To properly cover our subject, we do need to discuss the possible negative elements as well. Unhealthy compounds can be formed during smoking, and they can be incorporated into the finished malt as well as the final beer. For the homebrewer, awareness of these compounds and the methods by which they can be minimized only makes sense. And for the professional brewer whose products might come under regulatory scrutiny at some time, careful consideration of these issues is clearly essential.

The two kinds of compounds we need to discuss here are polycyclic aromatic hydrocarbons (PAHs) and nitrosamines.

PAHs

Technically, the term *PAH* includes more than a hundred organic compounds composed of two or more carbon rings. Even though just a few of the members of this group are known to be hazardous, the term *PAH*—which includes all these compounds—is used to designate the undesirable substances that we want to avoid.

Most Americans know about PAHs because of their association with the prototypical American barbecue grill. Here, meat drippings hit hot coals and burn to produce PAHs that will travel as smoke to the food being cooked. Unfortunately, we cannot eliminate our exposure to PAHs by shutting down the backyard barby. For starters, it appears that PAHs occur in nearly all heat-processed foods. Indeed, one authority concludes, "in the heating or smoking of food . . . PAH formation is a standard fact of life" (Maga, 1988, p. 113). To make things worse, PAHs have also been found in *uncooked* foods such as lettuce, which acquire these compounds via environmental contamination.

Beyond food, most Americans are exposed to PAHs as a part of daily life. They are found in many common hydrocarbon-based substances including motor oil, creosote, mineral oil, waxes, and solvents. In addition, they are commonly found in the combustion products from nearly every complex organic fuel including gasoline, diesel fuel, coal, and, of course, wood.

PAHs are made up of multiple fused benzene rings and can be formed from organic substances as simple as glucose (Maga, 1988, p. 113). When a complex organic molecule like wood is burned, the production of PAHs is inevitable. The formation of PAHs appears to be temperature dependent. More than one source states that PAH formation is minimal at temperatures below about 400 °C (Maga, 1988, p. 116; Pigott, 1980, p. 98). Furthermore, researchers have demonstrated a linear increase in PAH formation between 400 °C and 1000 °C—the approximate temperature range at which fires burn (Maga, 1988, p. 115–116).

Because PAH molecules are fairly large, they generally exist in smoke in association with soot particles. By hitching a ride on these fine particulates, they can travel virtually anywhere that smoke goes—a fact that explains environmental contamination with PAHs.

Given this knowledge of PAHs and their formation, we can see the logic in the steps most often taken by commercial smoked-food producers. For starters, they keep the temperature of smoke generation low—around 400 °C or less. Second, they take steps to remove particulate matter from the smoke with various types of screens and traps. Third, they may increase the distance between the smoke source and the materials being smoked or use some other method of smoke cooling in order to increase the precipitation of soot and PAHs along the way (Maga, 1988, p. 118).

Some producers also use sophisticated combustion devices that keep temperatures low initially, increasing only when PAH-forming volatiles have already been removed. This technique is akin to how a flame progresses down a match stick, consuming the wood in basically two stages. The first stage begins with controlled heat that slowly starts the wood charring so that the volatiles are progressively driven off at as low a temperature as possible. As the temperature is increased, eventually mostly carbon is left and the volatile PAH precursors are gone. We are now at the second stage where the temperature increases to a glowing "flame" type of combustion.

For home production, the easiest of these commercial techniques is temperature reduction. There are various methods to achieve this. Moistening the wood and piling it on well-lit coals in a manner that allows the wood to char slowly is the easiest. Another method, which can be used concurrently, is controlling the airflow to the fire to keep it from getting too hot. This method is a little more tricky as you must ensure that enough air gets to the fire so as not to severely choke it, since this can create a creosotelike smoky character. These are practical techniques for keeping your smoke-generation temperatures cool.

Nitrosamines

Nitrosamines can be formed by the action of nitrite on secondary and tertiary amines as would be found through the use of sodium nitrite (a commonly used preservative) in bacon and other processed meats. But when it comes to malt and ultimately beer, nitrosamines result from the combination of nitrous oxides with the proteins in malt. This reaction takes place when green malt is kilned at the end of the malting process. The nitrous oxides (NOx) are formed when nitrogen from the air passes through the flame used to heat the kiln. These oxides of nitrogen react as free radicals with protein (made up of amines) to create a number of compounds generally termed *nitrosamines*. Studies during the late 1970s and early 1980s regularly found nitrosamines in finished beer (summarized in Mangino et al., 1981).

Since the time that nitrosamines were identified in malt and beer, commercial maltsters have modified their production processes to ensure safe levels in finished malt. One solution was to change to low NOx combustion sources that dramatically reduce the nitrous oxide content in combustion gases. Another was to switch to indirect heating of the kiln air by using coils heated by steam or electric power. A final solution was to add a carefully controlled amount of sulfur or sulfur dioxide to the fire or combustion gases in order to block the formation of nitrosamines in the malt without creating off-flavors in the finished product (Mangino et al., 1981).

Production of smoked malt requires direct contact of the combustion gases with the malt. As a result, there is some risk of nitrosamine production. Still, it appears that wood fires produce small amounts of NOx because they burn at much lower temperatures (400 to 1000 °C) than gas burners (1800 to 2000 °C). (NOx production rises slowly with increasing temperature up to about 1400 °C but jumps exponentially as temperatures continue to rise beyond that.) When smoking takes place over a fire with little or no flame and is therefore at the low end of the wood-fire temperature range, Ray believes there is little reason for further concern over nitrosamines.

To be absolutely certain, however, Geoff endorses the use of a number of commercially available home smokers. Some employ an electrical element to heat the wood to smoking temperatures, which are lower than can be achieved by direct fire. Others heat the wood chips with an external gas flame, using a design that prevents the gas-combustion fumes from entering the smoked air stream.

Clinging to the Malt

Once the smoke reaches the malt, it has to stick in some way if we are going to get any smoke flavor into our finished beers. Fortunately, this happens pretty readily—especially with wet malt.

Smoke is actually deposited on the surface of the malt though a combination of effects. One is condensation of smoke compounds on the surface of the malt. The malt surface is cooled by evaporation during smoking, and as a result, the malt is cooler than the smoke. This cooling prompts condensation of the smoke on the malt, much as your breath condenses on a cold window.

Second, water-soluble components of smoke hit the wet surface of the malt and dissolve in the surface moisture. From here, they can be absorbed into the wet grain. Many of the key smoke-flavor compounds are volatile water-soluble organic compounds, so this absorption is a significant mode of flavoring for the malt.

Putting It All Together

In this chapter, we have explored the chemistry of wood and its destruction through burning. As with much of beer chemistry, we have found a complex collection of processes and reactions that make up the simple act that we think of as smoking.

We want to close this chapter by reviewing the most important elements of wood and smoke chemistry. When considered as a whole, they can help to guide you in the practical aspects of smoking that we consider in the next chapter. Here's what we see as the key issues:

- Hemicellulose, cellulose, and lignin all pyrolyze at different temperatures ranging from 200 to 400 °C (Guillen and Ibargoitia, 1996).
- The ratio of volatile compounds to char depends upon the temperature at which pyrolysis takes place.
- The quantity and type of *flavor* compounds present in the smoke depend on the nature of the wood and the temperature at which the smoke is generated (Guillen and Ibargoitia, 1996).

- The temperatures at which phenols (from lignins) are produced are generally higher than the temperatures that produce carbonyl derivatives (from cellulose and hemicellulose) (Guillen and Ibargoitia, 1996).
- A smoldering fire that lacks a flame will give off products that are less oxidized and more complex whereas a flaming burn will further oxidize volatiles into components that have a simpler chemistry and are more oxidized.
- Production of unhealthy polycyclic aromatic hydrocarbons (PAHs) begins to occur to a significant extent at about 400 °C. PAHs are fairly large molecules with lower volatility. They typically are found in high concentrations on soot particulates. Removal of these smoke particulates significantly lowers the level of PAH in smoke.
- Formation of nitrosamines may occur to a significant degree in malt when it is exposed to nitrous oxides formed by high-heat flames.

In some cases, we feel that this data point us in contradictory directions with regard to the practical aspects of smoking. But remember that these are only the facts that we know. The outcomes from smoking also rely on a wide range of factors that have yet to be definitively mapped including air humidity, draft volume, wood species, and wood seasoning, to name a few.

Yet despite the shortcomings of knowledge in this area suffered by the collective food technology, chemistry, and environmental scientists of the world, people manage to make good-tasting smoke-flavored beers. We believe that the knowledge presented in this chapter will help us all to make smoked beers that are better to drink and better for our health.

CHAPTER 5

Smoking Malt

Imparting a smoked character to malt on a small scale can be done in innumerable ways. What we list for you here are just a few that we have seen used successfully. We describe three small-scale methods to illustrate how varied the smoking methods can be. We have experimented with all three methods. In two of these methods, we have used commercially available smokers with completely different heating and smoking configurations. We also used different wood moistures, different base malts to smoke, and different amounts of moisture on the malts in each of our examples. All of this variety should help illustrate the range of experimentation that you can employ in your own process. The first two methods describe techniques that have been used in producing award-winning beers; the third is a convenient combination of both. Although you may not be able to implement any one of these to the letter, they can serve as guide in the development of your own approach to smoking malt.

We urge you to experiment with malt smoking. Properly dried smoked malts retain their smoked character during storage, although you will see some decline in potency after a few months. Smoke your malts by using different procedures and compare the intensity and character of the resulting products. Below are some tips to get you started. The wonderful thing about this flavor component is that everyone is familiar with it. And although you are not necessarily used to it in beer (yet!), you still will know what you like. Do not be intimidated by it.

One very easy way of experimenting with smoked-malt flavors, without having to make a batch of beer, is to take malt that you have smoked or smoked malt that you have purchased and mix it with hot water. The resulting "tea," when cooled to room temperature, will give you a quick analysis of the smoke flavors that you are dealing with.

The commercially available smoked malt from Weyermann is suitable for use as a base malt and may constitute a significant part of the grist for a recipe. The peat-smoked malt from Bairds, on the other hand, should only be a small part of your total grist charge. The commercial examples have a large range of smoke intensities. When we smoke malt on a small scale for our own use, the resulting product can also have quite a range of intensity. However, the techniques described here produce more intensely smoked malts, often with some roasted characteristics, and should be used as you would other specialty malts. Thus, self-smoked malt is generally designed to serve as only a small portion of your total grist charge.

Our historical research highlights the fact that smoke characters can easily overwhelm the beer. Many references point this out, so in developing your own technique for making smoked beer, it is best to start with the mindset of trying to *under*state the smoke characters. Let your first batch be the guide. Smoke is a wonderful background note, so do not fear that you are being too subtle. On the next batch you can always increase the intensity. Also, keep in mind that your palate easily becomes saturated with smoke, so as you brew with the smoked malt you will stop noticing the smoke aroma. If you are developing a recipe, remain mindful of your objectives.

Regardless of which of the three described smoking methods you choose to use, there are some general guidelines that you should follow when smoking malt. Let's review these overall guidelines before getting into the specifics of the different smoking techniques.

Any Water You Use Must Be Pure Water Completely Free of Any Chlorine

Distilled water is highly recommended. However, carbon-filtered water is an acceptable alternative if it removes the form of chlorine used in your water supply. Removing all chlorine is critical because chlorine reacts with the good-tasting phenols in the smoke, giving the beer an unpleasant medicinal taste. The phenols react with the chlorine to create substances that have flavor thresholds 100 to 1,000 times lower than just phenols, and the nature of how they taste changes from pleasantly smoky to an intense flavor similar to that of a Band-Aid™. *All of the water*, malt, and what you use in brewing must be chlorine free.

Use Any Wood That Is Appropriate for Smoking Food

Most of the classic smoking hardwoods are available and can be found easily as chips. Some commonly used hardwoods are apple, alder, hickory, mesquite, and maple. All these woods have been traditionally used to smoke foods. Be aware that because of this history, you will likely have flavor associations with certain foods. Many people associate hickory with ham, maple with sausage, or alder with fish, and consumers will identify it with your beer as well. This association is usually all right, but you'll want to keep it in mind. Apple is a nice mellow wood to try your first time out. Steer clear of pine! Pines and other conifers release a class of compounds called terpenes that are very unpleasant tasting. Also, bark is best removed from any wood source as there are resins concentrated in the bark that tend to produce a more acrid and harsh smoke. Once you are comfortable with using smoked malt in brewing, be inventive—what local smoke source is from your area? Some of the common woods discussed are obvious choices to smoke malt:

Beech is the traditional wood of the Bamberg smoked beers.

Apple is considered by some to be one of the best woods for smoking as it is mild and very pleasant without acrid notes.

Oak has been used in making malt supposedly in recent times in Poland and Scotland. Oak was used historically as a fuel (Steel, 1878, p. 22).

Alder adds a rich woody flavor and is traditionally used in the Northwest for smoking fish. It is used in many of the northern climates from Sweden to Alaska (Nordland, 1969, p. 30).

Mesquite is high in the same phenols as wheat beer, and so it is thought to be a nice complementary wood in this style of beer.

Hickory has been traditionally used in the United States with such a recognizable flavor that beers made with malt smoked with it are often reminiscent of ham or bacon. It is reported that hickory can have harsher phenolic character.

Some less common fuels include both the traditional and the unusual:

Peat is critical for the manufacture of whisky malt, and some commercial malt manufacturers make this flavor available. It typically comes in a variety of strengths:

low (5 ppm), medium (10 ppm), and high (15 ppm) phenolic content. Suggested use rate is rather low: 2 to 5 percent of the grist charge for a low to medium phenolic content. The result is quite intense, and its use is easily overdone—which will adversely affect the positive quality you desire. However, as a background flavor note, peat is very easy to use and quite effective.

Straw is a very pure cellulose source. For many centuries, straw was the preferred fuel probably owing to its low cost and acceptable smoke constituents.

Juniper is a traditional fuel even though its use as a wood source for smoking fuel tends to run counter to most smoking-fuel generalizations, as it is a soft wood. Juniper is even referenced as a fuel enhancement in the making of Scottish peated malt (Nordland, 1969, p. 30).

Possibly surprising fuels include ***coconut shells,*** which is supposed to give a very pleasant smoke flavor (Maga, 1988, p. 80). ***Hazel bushes*** have been used by some as a fuel for smoking (Nordland, 1969, p. 29). ***Corncobs*** have been used in the northeastern United States for smoking meat and were also found to be very mild and pleasant for smoking malt. ***Thistle*** is a very common, tall-growing plant (all right, a [useful] weed) that is high in cellulose. And finally, there are many other possibilities, for example, *maple, peach, orange, grapefruit, grapevine, cherry, sassafras, walnut, birch, elm, aspen, cottonwood, willow, balsam poplar, white ash,* and *bamboo.*

Every wood or smoke source is different, and you will need to experiment. For example, more or less water on the wood can make a profound change in the amount and character of phenols produced. It is a matter of trial and error to find the right combination of techniques to generate the best flavors from your fuel. Small changes in the way you generate smoke can have large effects on the quality of the smoke, so have patience and try variations on these techniques. There aren't hard and fast rules for every fuel source. Talk to your local commercial smokehouse operator for insights.

Be Safe

Obviously you are dealing with malt that can ignite during smoking and during drying. But what we really mean by "be safe" is more about producing the proper healthy smoke flavors and reducing the opportunity for any unwanted combustion products from getting into the smoked malt. The two classes of compounds we need to be mindful of are PAHs (polycyclic aromatic hydrocarbons) and nitrosamines (both are discussed in chapter 4). These same issues apply to all grilled foods, and malt is no more or less susceptible.

It is actually very easy to smoke your malt safely.

1. Use a steady, relatively cool fire or heat source to burn your "smoking" fuel—glowing coals without flames or an electrical element. If the heat source is an adjustable gas flame, you would not want the combustion gases from the smoking-fuel flames to touch the malt.

2. Protect the malt in a manner that prevents ash and tars from contacting or mixing with the malt. A slow, steady fire mainly from coals, will not kick up ash. By strategic use of stainless steel or copper screens in each of the methods, which we explain in the next section, we have been able to reduce the ash and prevent the condensing tars from getting mixed in with the malt. The screen acts as an ash filter, but also as a baffle to slow the smoke currents and allow the ash to fall out. The mesh size needs to be small but not so small as to clog up with tars, which condense on the screen's surface. By using two layers of 16 × 16 mesh, you will accomplish this objective. Stainless-steel or copper screen is recommended and can be purchased from hardware stores, specialty metal

fabricators, or mail-order companies such as Graingers (telephone (425) 251-5030; or Mcmaster-Carr (telephone (562) 692-5911; e-mail la.sales@mcmaster.com).

Smoke Enough Malt to Do Several Batches

The best way to develop a smoked-beer recipe is to be able to try different amounts of the same smoked malt in several batches. That way you can add more or less smoked character and easily adjust the recipe as you go. Smoked malt, when dried correctly, can be stored for quite a while. Once you have the beer recipe you like, then you'll want to begin figuring out how to adjust or control the actual smoke imparted into the malt during the smoking process. This is the challenge for the commercial brewer wishing to replicate his or her brew consistently.

Dry the Malt Thoroughly After Smoking

If after smoking, your malt is still damp, dry it in the oven at a very low temperature with the oven door open. Below 200 °F (93 °C) is fine. There are two reasons for this. First, drying the malt to a bone-dry state allows you to store the grain without fear of its developing mildew or stale characters. And second, this drying process removes the acetic acid (vinegar) that comes from wood pyrolysis. Acetic acid is something you will be able to taste in the beer as a bite, and it is not a pleasant or appropriate flavor in most styles of beer. By drying the malt, you can volatize off the acetic acid. Store the smoked malt in an airtight container after it is dry.

Sample Your Smoked Malt

As we have said, you can assess the character and intensity of your smoked malt, or commercially prepared malt, by making a "tea" from the malt soaked in hot water. Pour one cup of smoked malt into two cups of hot water (140 °F [60 °C]). Let the malt soak for 10 minutes, stir, and after it cools to room temperature, strain off the liquid for tasting. Although you can smell and taste it hot, tasting it at room temperature gives the best insight as to the overall affect on the palate. When you taste the tea, the smoke should be evident and pleasant. If it is not a good aroma, try changing your smoking regime for your malt. Though the flavor may be mild in the tea, it will be much more evident in the beer, because this tea-making process just dissolves some of the smoke flavors from the surface of the grains as compared to actually mashing the crushed smoked grains. In addition, the carbonation in the final beer will help release the smoke aromas. Keep in mind that your palate gets saturated with smoke very quickly. On the day you smoke the malt, your palate will be saturated, so do not try this test then, as you will have to let your olfactory senses recover from the day's smoking.

Use the Smoked Malt Sparingly the First Time You Brew with It

Smoke flavors and aromas are very powerful, but also tend to blind your palate. The first time you brew, use less smoked malt than you think will be necessary. We provide recommended grist proportions for each of the three smoking methods explained below. If after the first batch of beer you feel you don't have enough smoke flavor, add more smoked malt to the next batch. Keep in mind that once you've tasted the smoked malt or mash, you will have temporarily saturated your palate, and you may think you need to increase your usage. Do not fall into that trap! Also the recipe for the beer should be able to stand on its own, and although the intention is to have a smoke character in it, the beer style being brewed should still be true to that style. Smoked malt merely adds another dimension. And, even at very low levels of smoke, you should still have a nice beer. Relax, sit back, and enjoy.

Ok, let's do some smoking.

Method 1: Wet Smoking Chips and Wet Malt

The first method of making smoked malt that we discuss uses damp wood and a low combustion temperature to create a dense smoke, along with heat to partially dry and roast the grain. The method also uses wet malt; the water allows the smoke characters to be picked up by the malt during smoking.

Geoff has used a small home smoker that has an electrical element on a bed of rocks; the smoker also has racks to hold the malt. The appliance Geoff used was a Brinkmann Gourmet Electric Smoker, but many home smokers are of this basic style and can be used in essentially the same way. In comparison to some of the other models, however, this particular model has a larger area for holding wood chips, which we especially liked. It took only two hours to toast, roast, and smoke 5 pounds of malt on this smoker. We used pale malt, but by the time we were finished, it had turned an amber-hued color. After removing the malt from the smoker,

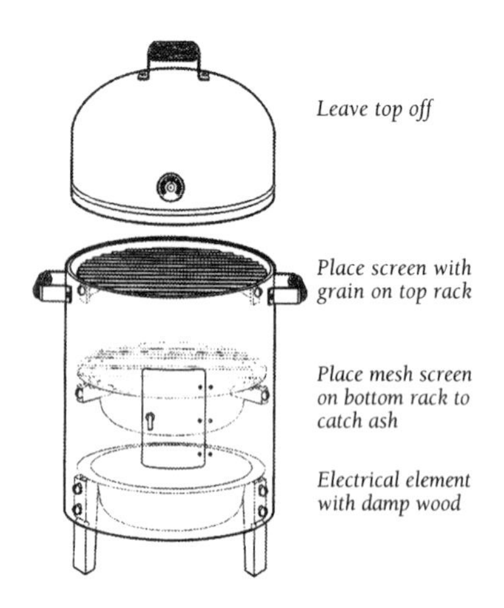

Brinkmann Electric Smoker

the grain needed an additional 36 hours to dry completely. We therefore finished the drying by placing the smoked malt on the 180 °F (82 °C) surface of a hot-water tank for two days, open to the air. As stated previously, this step is important for storage and to remove the acetic acid produced from wood pyrolysis. Here are the exact procedures:

Step 1: Wet 1.75 pounds of wood chips with 3 cups of distilled water and let the wood fully absorb the water. The real objective is to get the moisture level of the wood up so that you do not get any flames coming from the wood, just smoldering chips. If you are dealing with large chips (3 to 6 cm), it may take overnight; if you are dealing with small chips (1 to 3 cm), it may take only 1 hour for adequate absorption. Regardless of size, the chips can be wetted a few days in advance just to make sure the water has been totally absorbed and the chips are uniformly moist. Place the damp chips in the smoker in the bottom chamber made for them. This chamber contains the heating element that will start them smoldering. *Do not start the chips to smoldering until everything is set up.*

Step 2: Place a fine metal screen (15 to 24 mesh; stainless steel is best) on the lowest rack of the smoker. This screen will act as your ash catcher. If there is only one rack in your smoker, you can simply suspend from it a screen that covers the entire smoke path above the smoldering wood, but hangs at least 15 cm below the malt to be smoked. The screen acts somewhat as a filter but just as importantly as a baffle that slows and disperses the smoke to reduce migration of the ash and tar to the malt. *No matter how many racks you have, they should be very clean.*

Step 3: The top rack is where the malt is smoked. On this top rack, place another screen of copper or stainless steel that overlaps the entire open top. Mold the screen so that a 3-inch depth of moist malt can be held. This way, the heat and smoke will have to go up through the malt without any option for the smoke to bypass the malt. *Now there should be two layers of screen between the smoke source and the malt.* During smoking, the top of the smoker is left off, and the heat and smoke just pass through the grain.

Step 4: Place 5 pounds of pale malt and 3 cups of distilled water in a water-tight container, and then shake the container to wet all the malt evenly. *The malt should be* *wet only 15 minutes before starting the smoker.* Spread the malt evenly across the screen, leaving no clear spot through which the smoke and heat can escape without passing through the malt. This procedure will create a malt layer about 3 inches thick on an 18-inch diameter smoker screen.

Step 5: Start the heating element and let the chips smoke until they are totally consumed. This should take about 2 hours. *Do not disturb the chips by looking at their progress,* as this will waste a lot of heat and smoke. *The top should be left off of the smoker* so that the heat and smoke rise through the grain layer without the heat concentrating in the smoker and raising the temperature of the malt too high.

Step 6: After all the wood chips have been burned, take the screen of malt off of the smoker and dry it gently in a low-temperature oven or similar warm spot. To dry the grain, we suggest putting it in an oven, left slightly open, and set at less than 200 °F (93 °C) until the grain is dry. Be mindful that this part of the process could be a fire hazard. *Do not put the malt very close to the heating element of the stove or next to the direct fire of a gas oven during drying.* You must be careful not to let the grains catch fire. Remember that historically this danger was an issue, so let's not try to be historically nostalgic in this kilning exercise. Gentle drying, please! Do not worry about losing any smoke character during the drying process, as the smoke compounds that are on the grain are not as volatile as the water and acetic acid you are trying to drive off. Check the dryness of the malt before putting it away. The malt should be just as crisp and crunchy as the dry malt you started with. Then store it in an airtight container.

Critique: Using the "wet method" provides the maximum smoke pickup for your malt, and your smoked malt will go further as it is more intensely smoked. However, it is the slowest of the three processes we discuss. Smoked malt made from the wet method can be used at a level of 5 to 10 percent of the grist charge and will impart an obvious but pleasant smoke character.

Method 2: Dry Wood Chips and "Dry" Malt

The following method of smoking malt was adapted from the Vermont Pub and Brewery. When Geoff visited, they used a model of home smoker called a Cajun Cooker™. A grain basket comes with the Cajun Cooker, but if you use another similar smoker that doesn't have a grain basket or a different way of supporting the malt, you can contain the malt with a fine-mesh stainless steel screen (see the advice under method 1). The particular model used at the Vermont Pub and Brewery also has an external gas flame that heats a large tray where you can place wood in chip, chunk, or twig form. This heating method provides indirect gas heating of the wood to produce smoke; this heated smoke then wafts up to come in direct contact with the malt. At the Vermont Pub and Brewery, the malt smokers use one-third crystal and two-thirds pale malt, and they use a combination of woods: 60% apple twigs, 30% maple chips, and 10% hickory chips. Applewood enhances the fine aromatics and also adds flavor to the malt. It imparts a sweeter, more mellow smokiness. Since this is what Greg Noonan at Vermont Pub and Brewery is targeting in his smoked beer, this wood makes up the majority of the smoke source. However, maple and hickory make up the backbone of the smoke character. Maple imparts a strong flavor and aroma to malt. It is too overpowering and creosote-like to use alone, and it reminds people of sausage (which is commonly smoked with maple). The hickory adds a definite phenolic character, and it tends to remind people of smoked ham. The way this combination of woods is used in smoking is a bit analogous to hop use in the brewing process. The hickory and maple are used in the same way as high-alpha hops, and the apple is used as aromatic hops are.

The wood chips, chunks, or twigs are utilized dry, as no moistening of this varied smoke source is necessary. However, although we say the grains are "dry," the smoking method does require some slight misting of the grains with water during the smoking. Smoke deposition needs to have water available on the surface of the malt in order to condense effectively. But the grains are misted with only a couple of tablespoons of chlorine-free water, and within 15 minutes, the malt comes off the grill almost dry.

Step 1: Place 10 ounces of chips, chunks, or twigs in the bottom tray, directly above the gas heater. *Do not start the external heater until everything is set up and ready to go.* Woodchips or sawdust will generate a lot more smoke quickly as there is better contact with the heated surface, so a combination of chips and twigs could work fine. You could use a combination of different woods to blend the smoke elements from them.

Step 2: Place a fine metal screen (15 to 24 mesh; preferably stainless steel) below the rack where you will be smoking the malt. This screen should cover the entire smoke path above the smoldering wood, but should be a few inches below the malt to be smoked. This screen will act as an ash catcher.

Step 3: Make a smoke chimney by puncturing a tall metal coffee can with multiple holes. Put the hollow, perforated can in the middle of the grain basket or stainless steel screen. Place 10 to 15 pounds of malt in the grain basket. Mist the malt with 2 tablespoons of chlorine-free water. Stir the malt to uniformly disperse the water. ***Use less water during hotter, more humid months.*** Arrange the malt evenly around the "chimney" can. The grain should be to a level of about 1 inch below the top of the can. The perforated can allows smoke to pass up through the thick bed to reach the top of the grain mass.

Step 4: Start the gas and set the flame to a medium to low level. Once smoke starts wafting up, put the top on the smoker and let the heat and smoke pass through the grain. Wrap a moistened paper towel around the lid to act as a gasket to contain the smoke.

Step 5: After smoking for ten minutes, remove the cover, and you will notice moisture on top of the malt. Stir this moisture into the malt and leave the cover off while continuing to heat. Heat for an additional 5 to 7 minutes, which will aid in drying the malt. ***If you hear crackling, it means you are charring the malt, which is not desirable.*** This outcome could mean that your heat is too high or the smoking chips are used up.

Step 6: Turn off the gas heater and pull out the basket of grain. Empty the malt onto a sheet pan and spread out the malt evenly. The malt will be warm and relatively dry. Leave it on the sheet pan for at least 20 minutes and place in a warm spot to allow the malt to completely dry.

Critique: This "dry" method is a fast way of smoking grain. As you are adding much less moisture than in method 1, it is much easier to fully dry the grain after smoking. However, the issue of dryness becomes a critical control point in the process as ambient humidity and weather will play a much larger role in smoke pickup of the malt. The dry method produces a smoked character in malt that if used as 10–20 percent of the grist charge will impart an obvious but pleasant smoke character.

Method 3: Quick and Simple

The brewer who doesn't want to invest in a smoker can still achieve reasonable results. By using a backyard grill, we can impart the flavors of wood smoke quickly and create a smoked malt much like you would when grilling food to add smoked flavor. In this method—a combination of the "wet" and "dry" techniques from our first two methods is used.

Step 1: In a large Weber™ grill, build a charcoal briquette fire and let it burn down until you have about 4 cups of totally ash-covered coals. Bank the coals steeply on one side of the grill.

Step 2: Moisten 1 pound of wood chips with about 2 cups of water. You want the chips to be just barely damp. If you are using larger chunks, they will not pick up as much water but will work fine. Place the damp chips on the coals, heaping them high in the middle of the coals. Now place the grill over this smoking pile of chips as if you were ready to start cooking. Place a separate screen on the grill covering it entirely. This separates the smoke source from the malt. The screen will act as a baffle to catch most of the ash.

Step 3: On the opposite side of the grill, away from the coals, place a basket with a stainless-steel or copper screen (15 to 20 mesh) large enough to totally contain **and cover** 5 pounds of malt. The basket is used to allow quick removal of the grain, without burning or spilling! We also want to be sure that the grain doesn't touch the grill, since such backyard grills are often not totally cleaned of fats and oils from previous use and we don't want any cross contamination. The stainless-steel screen must be able to be folded over in a manner that totally envelopes the grain. This procedure keeps ash from falling into or mixing with the grain.

Smoking on the Weber Grill, with smoking materials in the foreground.

Step 4: Mist the grain lightly with about 2 tablespoons of chlorine-free water. Distilled water is best. Mix the grain and then fold the screen around the grain.

Step 5: Cover the grill, but make sure you let enough air into the grill to prevent the unpleasant creosote characters that can form if you choke the air to the coals down too much. However, conversely you cannot allow too much air, or it will make the chips flame up. We achieved the proper balance with the Weber grill by having the lower damper full open and the top vent full open, with the lid on tight.

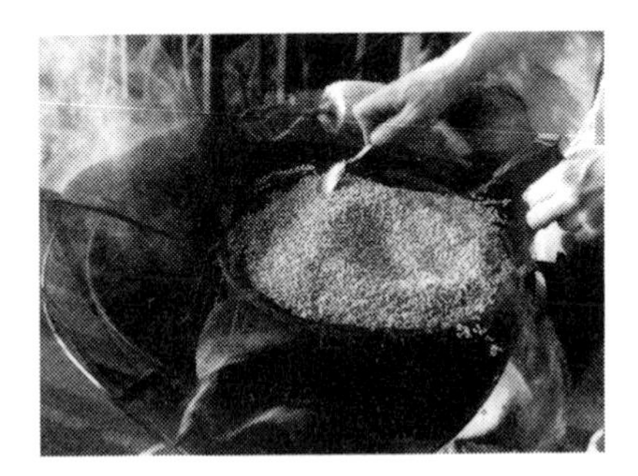

Misting the grain just as the smoke starts to rise from the Weber Grill. The copper screen will then be folded to completely cover the grain protecting it from ash.

Step 6: Smoke the malt for 10 minutes. Then stir the malt and then let it smoke for another 20 minutes. Replace the lid between smoking periods.

Step 7: Remove the grain, and spread it out on a tray in a warm place to cool and dry overnight.

Critique: This method is a fast way of smoking grain and can be modified for use on any type of grill. As the smoke is not forced through the grain, the results can vary greatly from grill to grill. This malt will impart an obvious but pleasant smoke character if used as 5 to 15 percent of the grist charge.

Summary

The methods described above are all different, yet each does a good job of producing a type of malt that can generate excellent smoke beers. These smoking methods by no means cover the range of methods you can employ; however, it does demonstrate some of the basic techniques. Use chlorine-free water at all times. Keep the ash from contaminating your malt and maintain a low, steady heat so that a hot flaming fire is not a part of the smoke generation. Make sure your final smoked malt product is bone dry for storage; the final drying step also assures that some of the unpleasant volatile compounds like acetic acid have been driven off.

Attaining a consistent smoked character from batch to batch is achievable. However, the best method of

Using Smoked Malt That Has Been Stored

Let's say the beer you brewed last year was made with 2 pounds of smoked malt out of a total malt bill of 10 pounds. You now want to brew a beer with the same smoke intensity one year later using some of the same smoked malt you had left over. As the smoked malt is one year old, it has lost some of its intensity. Therefore, you need to increase the smoked malt used in your recipe to 2.4 pounds (a 20 percent increase) out of the 10 pounds total.

developing a smoked-beer recipe by using your own smoked malt is to make enough malt for a number of batches. You can than adjust the recipes as you go if you want more or less smoked character. We suggest that you start by using the lower proportions of smoked malt, and then work up. Keep in mind that as the malt ages, it will mellow and lose some of its sharper characteristics. So after smoked malt has been stored for a year, the proportion of it in the grist will need to be increased by 20 percent or more in order to achieve the same results. Also, the smoke character in the finished beer will mellow with time. So if the smoke character is too intense, let the beer rest for a year and then try a bottle of it again.

Every smoke source is different, and some may not be suitable for beer or the style you are using it in. If you want to generate your own type of smoked malt, try woods that are commonly used in smoking foods, and you should be OK. You can have too much of a good thing, and smoke is a perfect example—too much and even the best smoke flavors become unpleasant. Again, it is a matter of trial and error to hit on an appealing smoked character in your beer.

CHAPTER 6

Brewing Smoked Beers

Over the years we have both enjoyed brewing smoked beers for our own consumption and to share with others. Despite this, our research for this book familiarized us with some new approaches to smoked beer brewing that widened our view of the field even further. As an example, Ray used to blend bottled rauchbier with bottled weizen occasionally to create a smoky-flavored German-style weizen beer. Nearly everyone who ever saw this thought it was crazy, but it tasted pretty good. Lo and behold, during our research in Bamberg, we found that smoke-flavored Bavarian-style weizen beers are a staple at the leading rauchbier pubs. And, we even found a U.S. brewpub—one of John Harvard's Brew Pubs—that makes a smoked weizenbock called Buckhead Smoked Weizenbock.

As a result of all these discoveries, the recipe section has grown considerably from what we originally thought it would be. At first, we figured there would be a smoked porter, a Bamberg-style beer, and then maybe a wee heavy to round things out. But as you will see, we have expanded well beyond these few favorites to include not only those beers with assertive smoked character, but also those that deliver an attractive maltiness with a very subtle complexity added by smoked malt.

Notes on the Recipe Assumptions

First, please note that these recipes cover a wide range of beer styles. In many cases, we cannot provide details on the proper production of specific styles like weizen, Scotch ale, and Pilsener. Here we must assume that the reader has some familiarity with production of these styles or will seek out other sources that can provide that knowledge. We recommend that you consult other volumes from the Classic Beer Style Series as well as Ray's *Designing Great Beers* in order to fill in the missing information.

Malt Bill Quantities: Homebrew (5 gallon) recipes are based on 75% brewhouse yield; commercial recipes are based on 80%.

Hops: All hop pellets for bitterness assume 31 percent utilization during a 60-minute boil. The targeted IBUs (International Bitterness Units) and equivalent HBUs (homebrew bittering units) are given for each recipe to facilitate adjustments.

Extract: Each recipe includes quantities of light malt extract that can be substituted for the main unsmoked malts. The quantities specified are based on an assumption of 36 SG/pound/gallon (points of specific gravity per pound of extract per gallon of wort) for syrup and 45 SG/pound/gallon for dry malt. *Note: The quantities for both syrup and dry malt are given for each recipe, but you should use one or the other, not both.*

Water: Most recipes are for amber-colored or darker beer and will be malt balanced. In general, you will want to use chlorine-free water. Then with only one or two exceptions, little else is required other than addition of sufficient calcium to achieve your desired mash chemistry. Many brewers use calcium chloride to provide a roundness that complements malt-balanced beers. Accordingly, Ray has routinely used calcium chloride in the making of many styles, including smoked beers. Geoff, on the other hand, is concerned about the potential for chloride interactions with smoke components and subsequent production of chloro-phenols as an off-flavor. Thus to be safe, you may wish to choose gypsum for calcium additions. Whichever you choose, the amount you add will depend on the chemistry of your water. In cases where other water issues are important, we have noted them in the recipe.

Yeasts: Many different yeasts will be appropriate for each recipe. We have listed recommended yeasts from the two suppliers that are currently most popular among small-scale brewers in the United States and therefore easiest to find in retail stores. Other yeast suppliers can certainly provide suitable strains for these recipes as well, and if you wish to use other suppliers, we're sure they will be more than happy to help you select a strain that is equivalent to the ones that we have recommended.

Stöffla

We've take the name—and the recipe—for this beer from the delightful quaff we enjoyed at the Drei Kronen in Memmelsdorf, just a few minutes from Bamberg. The recipe makes a very nice dunkel-style beer when done as a lager—and if left unfiltered, it will emulate the "keller" style as presented at Drei Kronen. At the same time, this beer can just as easily transform into a nice brown ale by the substitution of ale yeast.

Recipe

Malt	Extract 5 gal.	All-Grain 5 gal.	All-Grain 1 bbl.	All-Grain Grist Ratios
Pilsener	—	1 lb. (0.45 kg)	6.0 lb. (2.7 kg)	10%
Munich	—	4 lb.	23 lb. (10.4 kg)	38%
Liquid extract	4.0 lb. (1.8 kg)	—	—	
or	*or*	—	—	
Dry extract	3.25 lb. (1.5 kg)			
Weyermann smoked	4 lb. (1.8 kg)	4 lb. (1.8 kg)	23 lb. (10.4 kg)	38%
Cara-Hell	—	1 lb. (0.45 kg)	6.0 lb. (2.7 kg)	10%
Cara-Vienna or crystal 30	1 lb. (0.45 kg)			
pH malt	—	0.5 lb.	3 lb. (1.4 kg)	5%

Hops	Extract 5 gal.	All-Grain5 gal.	All-Grain1 bbl.
Bittering Hops			
Perle pellets (7.0% aa)	0.75 oz. (21 g)	0.75 oz. (21 g)	4.5 oz. (128 g)
HBUs	5.25	5.25	—
IBUs	25	25	25
Flavor Hops (20–30 minutes)			
Tettnanger (optional)	0.5 oz. (14 g)	0.5 oz. (14 g)	3 oz. (85 g)
Aroma Hops (2 minutes)			
Tettnanger (optional)	0.5 oz. (14 g)	0.5 oz. (14 g)	3 oz. (85 g)

Specifications:	
Target original gravity	1.055 (13.5 °P)
Final gravity	1.014 (3.5 °P)
Mash temperature	153 °F (67 °C)
Yeast	Bavarian lager for German-style dunkel; Chico or American ale for brown ale version
Alcohol by volume	About 5.4 percent

Ein Hauch von Rauch

This is a Pilsener-style beer with a "hint of smoke," similar to the Felsentrunk served at the Hartmann Brewery in Würgau. If you don't want to tackle the lagering, just ferment it with a clean ale yeast and serve it up as a Kölsch or cream ale. The important thing is to produce a pale, highly drinkable beer with just a touch of smoke as a secondary flavor characteristic.

Recipe

Malt	Extract 5 gal.	All-Grain 5 gal.	All-Grain 1 bbl.	All-Grain Grist Ratios
Pilsener	—	8 lb. (3.6 kg)	48 lb. (21.8 kg)	85%
Liquid extract	5.8 lb. (2.6 kg)			
or	*or*			
Dry extract	4.9 lb. (2.2 kg)			
Weyermann smoked	1 lb. (0.45 kg)	1 lb. (0.45 kg)	5.6 lb. (2.5 kg)	10%
Cara-Hell	—	0.5 lb. (0.225 kg)	2.8 lb. (1.3 kg)	5%

Hops	Extract 5 gal.	All-Grain5 gal.	All-Grain1 bbl.
Bittering Hops			
Tettnanger (4.5%)	1.5 oz. (42.5 g)	1.5 oz. (42.5 g)	10.0 oz. (283 g)
HBUs	6.75	6.75	—
IBUs	35	35	35
Flavor Hops (30 minutes)			
Tettnanger	1 oz. (28 g)	1 oz. (28 g)	6 oz. (170 g)
Aroma Hops (2 minutes)			
Saaz	1 oz. (28 g)	1 oz. (28 g)	6 oz. (170 g)

Specifications:	
Target original gravity	1.048 (12 °P)
Final gravity	1.010 (2.5 °P)
Water treatment	Reduce carbonate to less than 50 ppm; use gypsum for calcium additions.
Mash temperature	150 °F (65.5 °C)
Yeast	Bavarian or Munich lager. Ferment and condition under lager conditions. As an alternative, you can make this using Chico or American ale yeast. Ferment cool (65–70 °F [18–21 °C]) for a snappy cream-ale style beer.
Alcohol by volume	About 5.0 percent

The Kaiser's Lovely Dom

Okay, so this is a deliberately obscure name for a darkly opaque beer. Although inspired by the Meranier Schwarzbier (black lager) brewed by the Kaiserdom Brewery in Bamberg, it brings more smoke to the table. With 20 percent rauch malt, the smoke is clearly discernible, although far from overwhelming as it will mix with the roasted notes of the black malt. Of course you could knock back the smoke a bit more by exchanging Pilsener malt for a part of the smoked malt if you wish.

Recipe

Malt	Extract 5 gal.	All-Grain 5 gal.	All-Grain 1 bbl.	All-Grain Grist Ratios
Pilsener	—	7 lb. (3.2 kg)	42 lb. (19 kg)	70%
Liquid extract	5 lb. (2.3 kg)			
or	*or*			
Dry extract	4 lb. (1.8 kg)			
Weyermann smoked	2.25 lb. (1 kg)	2 lb. (0.9 kg)	12 lb. (5.4 kg)	20%
Carafa II or black	1 lb. (0.45 kg)	1 lb. (0.45 kg)	6 lb. (2.75 kg)	10%

Hops	Extract 5 gal.	All-Grain5 gal.	All-Grain1 bbl.
Bittering Hops			
Liberty 5.6%	1.25 oz. (35.4 g)	1.25 oz. (35.4 g)	7.0 oz. (198 g)
HBUs	7	7	—
IBUs	30	30	30
Flavor Hops (20 minutes)			
Liberty	0.25 oz. (7 g)	0.25 oz. (7 g)	1.5 oz. (42 g)
Aroma Hops (2 minutes)			
Liberty	0.25 oz. (7 g)	0.25 oz. (7 g)	1.5 oz. (42 g)

Specifications:	
Target original gravity	1.052 (13 °P)
Final gravity	1.012 (3 °P)
Mash temperature	151 °F (66 °C)
Yeast	Bavarian or Munich lager. Ferment and condition under lager conditions.
Alcohol by volume	About 5.25 percent

Bamberger Rauchbier

Here you go, smoke lovers. Although the smoke intensity in imported rauch malt may vary somewhat, this recipe will give you an unmistakable smokiness in the Bamberg style. Start here and fine-tune up or down to suit your tastes. Also, if you increase the quantities of Munich and smoked malt by 20% without changing the hopping rates, it should give you an enjoyable Rauchbock as well.

Recipe

Malt	Extract 5 gal.	All-Grain 5 gal.	All-Grain 1 bbl.	All-Grain Grist Ratios
Munich	—	5.5 lb. (2.5 kg)	30 lb. (13.6 kg)	50%
Liquid extract	3.5 lb. (1.6 kg)			
or	*or*			
Dry extract	2.8 lb. (1.3 kg)			
Weyermann smoked	5 lb. (2.3 kg)	5 lb. (2.3 kg)	30 lb. (13.6 kg)	50%
Cara-Munich or crystal 60	1 lb. (0.45 kg)			
Black or Carafa II	2 oz. (56 g)	2 oz. (56 g)	10 oz. (283 g)	1%

Hops	Extract 5 gal.	All-Grain5 gal.	All-Grain1 bbl.
Bittering Hops			
Tettnanger (4.5% aa)	1.375 oz. (39 g)	1.375 oz. (39 g)	8.5 oz. (240 g)
HBUs	6	6	—
IBUs	30	30	30
Aroma Hops (2 minutes)			
Tettnanger	0.25 oz. (7 g)	0.25 oz. (7 g)	1.5 oz. (42 g)

Specifications:	
Target original gravity	1.056 (13.9 °P)
Final gravity	1.014 (3.5 °P)
Mash temperature	Double decoction if possible, with a protein rest at 122 °F (50 °C) and saccharification at 154 °F (68 °C). Else infusion at 154 °F (68 °C).
Yeast	Bavarian or Munich lager. Ferment and condition under lager conditions.
Alcohol by volume	About 5.5 percent

Lightening Flash White Smoke Weizen

After drinking a few rauchbiers in Bamberg, one hardly notices the smoke character in the weizens made by the same brewers. Still smoke plays a significant role in this interpretation of the classic Bavarian wheat beer. Yeast selection and fermentation conditions will determine how much weizen character you get in the final beer, and those who prefer an American-style wheat can substitute the ale yeast of their choice as an alternative.

Recipe

Malt	Extract 5 gal.	All-Grain 5 gal.	All-Grain 1 bbl.	All-Grain Grist Ratios
Wheat malt	—	6.3 lb. (2.9 kg)	36 lb. (16.3 kg)	67%
Liquid wheat or weizen extract	5.1 lb. (2.3 kg)			
or	*or*			
Dry wheat or weizen extract	4.3 lb. (2.0 kg)			
Weyermann smoked	3.0 lb. (1.4 kg)	3.0 lb. (1.4 kg)	18 lb. (8.2 kg)	33%

Hops	Extract 5 gal.	All-Grain5 gal.	All-Grain1 bbl.
Bittering Hops			
Hersbrucker (4.0% aa)	0.85 oz. (24 g)	0.85 oz. (24 g)	5.5 oz. (156 g)
HBUs	3.4	3.4	—
IBUs	17	17	17

Specifications:	
Target original gravity	1.052 (13 °P)
Final gravity	1.016 (4 °P)
Mash temperature	152 °F (67 °C)
Yeast	Weizen yeast
Alcohol by volume	About 4.5 percent

Dyslexic Dunleavy's Knotwood Gargoyle Ale

Brewed around Christmas of 1993, this beer won Ray a third place in the Old Ale–Strong Ale category of the 1994 National Homebrew Competition as a wee heavy or strong Scotch ale. Like many American interpretations of Scotch ale, this one includes some smoke—although in this case, it comes from wood-smoked malt rather than the peat-smoked type. Nearly any ale with this kind of gravity built from such a wide range of malts will be deliciously complex. Here the smoked malt adds to the complexity, giving additional interest to a richly attractive quaff.

Recipe

Malt	Extract 5 gal.	All-Grain 5 gal.	All-Grain 1 bbl.	All-Grain Grist Ratios
Pale ale	—	11 lb. (5.0 kg)	62 lb. (28.1 kg)	59%
Liquid extract	8.5 lb. (3.85 kg)	—	—	
or	*or*			
Dry extract	6.75 (3.1 kg)			
Biscuit	1.5 lb. (0.7 kg)	1.5 lb. (0.7 kg)	8.8 lb. (4 kg)	9%
Crystal 80 L	1.25 lb. (0.6 kg)	1.25 lb. (0.6 kg)	7.4 lb. (3.35 kg)	7%
Weyermann smoked	1 lb. (0.45 kg)	1 lb. (0.45 kg)	6 lb. (2.7 kg)	6%
Cara-Pils	1 lb. (0.45 kg)	1 lb. (0.45 kg)	6 lb. (2.7 kg)	6%
Cara-Munich	1 lb. (0.45 kg)	1 lb. (0.45 kg)	6 lb. (2.7 kg)	6%
Special B	0.25 lb. (113 g)	0.25 lb. (113 g)	1.5 lb. (0.7 kg)	2%
Roast barley	1 oz. (28 g)	1 oz. (28 g)	0.4 lb. (180 g)	0%

Hops	Extract 5 gal.	All-Grain5 gal.	All-Grain1 bbl.
Bittering Hops			
Fuggles pellets (3.0% aa)	2.25 oz. (64 g)	2.25 oz. (64 g)	14 oz. (400 g)
HBUs	6.75	6.75	—
IBUs	25	25	25
Flavor Hops (15 minutes)			
Fuggles pellets	0.5 oz.	0.5 oz.	3 oz.

Specifications:	
Target original gravity	1.090 (21.5 °P)
Final gravity	1.032 (8 °P)
Mash temperature	156 °F (69 °C)
Yeast	Wyeast 1338—European ale
Alcohol by volume	About 7.5 percent

Brenner Strasse Mild

This dark English mild beer takes its name from the Bamberg street where you'll find the Weyermann Specialty Malting Company. This recipe was first brewed to share with Thomas and Sabine Weyermann who hosted our trips to Bamberg and contributed immeasurably to the research for this book. Ray shared this recipe with the Weyermann's and their staff at Brennerstraße where all found it to be a suitable accompaniment for weiss wurst on a chilly day. Of course it is made exclusively with Weyermann malts!

Directions for Homemade Malts

The starting point for both smoked brown malt and oven-toasted amber malt can be any pale-ale malt that you have on hand. Use your favorite smoking procedure from Chapter 5 to make the brown malt—just be sure to leave it on the smoker until a reasonable amount of color has developed.

Recipe

Malt	Extract 5 gal.	All-Grain 5 gal.	All-Grain 1 bbl.	All-Grain Grist Ratios
Light Munich	—	5.0 lb. (2.25 kg)	28 lb. (12.7 kg)	62%
Liquid extract	3.75 lb. (1.7 kg)	—	—	
or	*or*			
Dry extract	3.0 lb. (1.4 kg)			
Weyermann smoked	2 lb. (0.9 kg)	2 lb. (0.9 kg)	12 lb. (5.4 kg)	26%
Cara-Munich III	10 oz. (285 g)	10 oz. (285 g)	3.5 lb. (1.6 kg)	8%
Carafa II	5 oz. (135 g)	5 oz. (135 g)	1.8 lb. (0.8 kg)	4%

Hops	Extract 5 gal.	All-Grain5 gal.	All-Grain1 bbl.
Bittering Hops			
Willamette (3.9% aa)	1.75 oz. (50 g)	1.75 oz. (50 g)	11.5 oz. (325 g)
HBUs	6.825	6.825	—
IBUs	25	25	25
Flavor Hops (10 minutes)			
Liberty	0.25 oz. (7 g)	0.25 oz. (7 g)	1.5 oz. (42 g)

Specifications:	
Target original gravity	1.040 (10 °P)
Final gravity	1.008 (2 °P)
Mash temperature	150 °F (65.5 °C)
Yeast	Wyeast Irish Ale
Alcohol by volume	About 4.2 percent

Ray's Pyroliginous Malt-Pop Porter

Like most homebrewers who love smoked beer, Ray has tried his hand at making smoked porter a number of times over the years. This one was cooked up with home-made brown and amber malts, and the original was served to the throngs at the Southern California Homebrewers Festival in Temecula one year. This version calls for smoked brown malt and oven-toasted amber malt to yield a roasty-toasty smoked-porter treat.

Make the amber malt in the oven following these directions: Place pale-ale malt to a depth of ½ inch in a foil lined cooking pan. Be sure to keep several kernels of the malt outside the oven for comparison. Cook in the oven as follows: for 45 minutes at 230 °F (110 °C), then 20 to 60 minutes at 300 °F (149 °C). After the first 20 minutes of this cycle, cut several toasted and untoasted kernels in half to inspect the color of the starchy endosperm. For amber malt, the interior area should be "light buff" in color when finished. Continue heating at 300 °F (149 °C) until this color is achieved, usually after 45 to 50 minutes.

Recipe

Malt	Extract 5 gal.	All-Grain 5 gal.	All-Grain 1 bbl.	All-Grain Grist Ratios
Pale ale	—	3.75 lb. (1.7 kg)	22 lb. (10 kg)	33%
Liquid extract	3.0 lb. (1.4 kg)	—	—	
or	*or*			
Dry extract	2.5 lb. (1.1 kg)			
Homemade amber	3.75 lb. (1.7 kg)	3.75 lb. (1.7 kg)	22 lb. (10 kg)	33%
Homemade brown	3.75 lb. (1.7 kg)	3.75 lb. (1.7 kg)	22 lb. (10 kg)	33%

Hops	Extract 5 gal.	All-Grain5 gal.	All-Grain1 bbl.
Bittering Hops			
Galena (11.7% aa)	0.75 oz. (21 g)	0.75 oz. (21 g)	4.5 oz. (128 g)
HBUs	8.8	8.8	—
IBUs	40	40	40
Flavor Hops (20 minutes)			
Kent Goldings	1 oz. (28 g)	1 oz. (28 g)	6 oz. (170 g)

Specifications:	
Target original gravity	1.056 (13.8 °P)
Final gravity	1.022 (2 °P)
Mash temperature	155 °F (68 °C)
Yeast	Any British ale yeast
Alcohol by volume	About 4.5 percent

Grätzer

This one is definitely in the category of "experimental beers"—we wouldn't recommend brewing up 15 gallons on the first try, much less 15 barrels at the local brewpub! This low-alcohol, smoky, bitter style was quite popular in what is now Poland as recently as 100 years ago. Some producers apparently made it with an all-wheat malt grist, but we have put in 50 percent Pils malt to ease mashing. Those with a real spirit for adventure can try the 100% wheat approach.

For best results, smoke your own wheat over oak wood and then give it a go. Alternately, you could substitute Weyermann smoked malt for the Pilsener malt and use regular wheat malt. The result wouldn't be authentic, but it would be an interesting first stab at the style and might inspire you to further experimentation.

Recipe

Malt	Extract 5 gal.	All-Grain 5 gal.	All-Grain 1 bbl.	All-Grain Grist Ratios
Pils	—	3 lb. (1.4 kg)	15.25 lb. (6.9 kg)	50%
Liquid extract	2.0 lb. (0.9 kg)	—	—	
or	*or*			
Dry extract	1.6 lb. (0.75 kg)			
Oak-smoked wheat malt	3.0 lb. (1.4 kg)	3 lb. (1.4 kg)	15.25 lb. (6.9 kg)	50%

Hops	Extract 5 gal.	All-Grain5 gal.	All-Grain1 bbl.
Bittering Hops			
Saaz (4% aa)	1.5 oz. (42 g)	1.5 oz. (42 g)	10 oz. (300 g)
HBUs	6	6	—
IBUs	30	30	30

Specifications:	
Target original gravity	1.028 (7 °P)
Final gravity	1.012 (3 °P)
Mash temperature	158 °F (70 °C)
Yeast	Wyeast 1338—European Ale Yeast
Alcohol by volume	About 3.7 percent

Millennium Rauchbock

This beer was created by Martin Zarnkow and Kornel Vetterlein at Weihenstephan University in Germany to commemorate the coming of the year 2000. It displays a spicy-sweet nose with just a hint of smoke. The palate is fairly light given the OG, but rich with malt flavor. Smoke is evident if you are looking for it, pretty subtle otherwise. Long lagering makes this incredibly smooth and alluringly easy to drink. Melanoidin malt is a German specialty malt similar to an American product called Special Roast. If you cannot find either of these products, substitute a dark Munich malt instead. Also, the original recipe used Orion hops, but I have substituted Northern Brewer due to their wider availability in the US.

Recipe

Malt	Extract 5 gal.	All-Grain 5 gal.	All-Grain 1 bbl.	All-Grain Grist Ratios
Pilsner	—	6.5 lb. (3 kg)	38 lb. (17.2 kg)	41%
Liquid extract	4.5	—	—	
or	*or*			
Dry extract	3.8			
Weyermann Rauch	3 lb. (1.4 kg)	3 lb. (1.4 kg)	15 lb. (6.8 kg)	19%
Melanoidin	0.75 lb. (0.33 kg)	0.75 lb. (0.33 kg)	4 lb. (1.8 kg)	5%
Roasted Rye	0.25 lb (113 gm)	0.25 lb (113 gm)	1.25 lb (0.57 kg)	1.5%
Dark Wheat Malt	3.75 lb (1.7 kg)	3.75 lb (1.7 kg)	19 lb (8.6 kg)	24%
CaraPils	1.5 lb (0.7 kg)	1.5 lb (0.7 kg)	7.5 lb (3.4 kg)	9.5%

Hops	Extract 5 gal.	All-Grain5 gal.	All-Grain1 bbl.
Bittering Hops			
Northern Brewer (8% aa) first wort hopping	0.5 oz. (14 g)	0.5 oz. (14 g)	2.5 oz. (71 g)
Northern Brewer (8% aa) ninety minutes	0.5 oz. (14 g)	0.5 oz. (14 g)	2.5 oz. (71 g)
Hersbrucker (4% aa) Steeped at end of boil or in whirlpool	0.5 oz. (14 g)	0.5 oz. (14 g)	2.5 oz. (71 g)
HBUs	10	10	—
IBUs	30	30	30

Specifications:	
Target original gravity	1.076 (18.4 °P)
Final gravity	1.014 (3.5 °P)
Mash temperature	Mash in at 100 °F (38 °C) and raise to 125 °F (52 °C) for 30 minutes. Raise to 144 °F (62 °C) for 60 minutes, then 162 °F (72 °C) for 60 minutes and finally 172 °F (78 °C) for 10 minutes.
Yeast	White Labs WLP830—German Lager Yeast
Alcohol by volume	About 7.5 percent

APPENDIX A

The Joy of Cooking with Smoked Beer

Cooking with beer? Absolutely! Beer is food after all (consider its healthy ingredients and marvelous flavors), and has long been used in the kitchen. While some of us may think of familiar classic beer recipes such as Welsh Rarebit or *Carbonnade a la Flamandes*, there is a (smoked) world to discover. In some countries, for example Belgium, cooking with beer is a national gastronomic specialty!

The range of beer use in cooking is quite broad—from simply using it as the liquid base for soups, to reductions for use in desserts. Beer may add only a subtle accent to the dish, or it may be a primary flavor component to the recipe. Generally speaking, beers are slightly acidic, have dissolved sugars and proteins, and have a bitter component coming from hops. Hop bitterness is similar to the bitterness found in many herbs used in the kitchen, which is why hops are called the spice of beer. The delicate aromatic nature of beer comes from malt, hops, and yeast. Each style has its own signature aroma, flavor, and aftertaste. We suggest these outstanding books on cooking with beer: *The Great American Beer Cookbook*, by Candy Schermerhorn (Brewers Publications, 1995); *Stephen Beaumont's Brewpub Cookbook*, by Stephen Beaumont (Brewers Publications, 1998); and ***Ultimate Beer*** by Michael Jackson.

Following are a few general tips that apply to using beer in cooking, and that will whet your appetite for foods made with smoked flavored beers.

- Smoked beer makes a great marinade. It is slightly acidic (as are all beers) and therefore will tenderized meat in the process. Use beer and spices to marinate seafood, beef or wild game overnight before cooking the next day. Try substituting beer for all or part of a liquid in a recipe—even in pancakes (they float with lightness)!

- Pair heavier beers like smoked stouts and smoked porters with more robust foods, and lighter flavored beers like a smoked *weiss* and or smoked amber lager with more delicately flavored dishes.
- Reducing beer concentrates the flavors, including the bitterness of hops. You may want to adjust the recipe to add fruit, cream, or something with a touch of sweetness to balance the increased bitterness of the hops.
- Add a dash or a bottle of beer to finish off a soup, stew or sauce.
- Use smoked beer to deglaze a pan—smoke will compliment the "roasted" flavors.
- Steam or poach seafood with a smoked beer and combination of spices.
- Beer used early in the preparation will most likely not contribute to the aroma, but added just before serving will give sublime aromatic character to the dish.

And now, off to the kitchen to prepare one of the following mouth-watering recipes. ***Bon appetit!***

Smoked Porter Salmon Spread

From: Perch Restaurant
Denali National Park, Alaska
Created by Leslie LeQuire

This is a wonderful appetizer to enjoy with friends.

1	lb. cream cheese, room temperature
5-8	oz. smoked salmon
1	tsp Old Bay® Seasoning (or comparable substitute)
1	Tbsp fresh parsley, finely chopped
2	Tbsp minced onion, fresh or dried
1/3	cup Smoked Porter

Blend all ingredients in a food processor or blender. Refrigerate overnight. Serve with fresh beer bread—or any great bread—or crackers.

Crab and Linguini Leopold

From: Rogue's Brewers-on-the-Bay Restaurant
South Beach, Oregon
Created by Chef Kurt Eisler

After a great day of crabbing on the Oregon coast, you've probably come home with some Dungeness crab! What better way to complement the crab you grabbed than in this marvelous recipe with linquini. Serves 4.

4	oz. Dungeness crab (or any crab meat)
1	lb. linquini
2	oz. white wine
2	oz. salted butter
1	large roma tomato, diced
6	mushrooms, finely sliced

1 Tbsp chopped garlic
1 tsp salt
1 tsp pepper
1/2 lemon
2 oz. Parmesan cheese, finely grated
2 cups smoked beer

In a large pot, bring 4 quarts of water to a boil. Add the linquini, broken in half, and cook till al dente.

In a large sauté pan, combine the butter, garlic, wine, tomato, mushrooms, salt and pepper. Sauté for about 4 minutes. Add smoked beer and the cooked pasta, and reduce liquid by a third.

At the very end, add the crab, lemon, and parmesan to the pasta, toss, heat, and serve. Don't forget the garlic bread and your favorite salad.

Brewmaster's Marinated Black Cod

From: Alaskan Brewing Company
Juneau, Alaska
Created by Brewmaster, Geoff Larson, for "our annual company cookoff"

Black Cod is high in oil and soft in texture. Honey and soy sauce were used to firm up the flesh without drying it. I added anise, mace, and fennel to the marinade, allowing the sweet aroma to mingle with the contrasting bitterness and astringency of the Smoked Porter. The result is that the tender black cod, nicknamed butterfish, seems to melt in your mouth. Serves 8-10 (these are large fish). Bon appetit!

4 Black cod filets
24 oz. (1 1/2 bottles) Smoked Porter
24 oz. (3 cups) soy sauce
12 oz. honey

1	Tbsp ground mace
8	bay leaves
1/4	tsp anise seed
1/4	tsp fennel seed
1/4	tsp white pepper

To prepare the marinade, mix together the liquid and dry ingredients, and warm on the stove until hot. DO NOT BOIL. Let the marinade sit at room temperature for one hour, then chill in the refrigerator. Pour all the marinade over the cod fillets, and let stand in the refrigerator for 24 hours, and not more than 48 hours. Remove from marinade and bake uncovered at 350 °F until the fish readily flakes apart. You may also broil or barbeque instead. Serve with hot, boiled, new red potatoes.

Sauerbraten Meatballs

From: Vermont Pub & Brewery
Burlington, Vermont

These are absolutely the best, and most unusual, meatballs you will ever eat! Who would think to use gingersnaps in a meatball recipe. ☺

1	lb. very lean ground beef
2/3	cup (about 12) crushed gingersnaps
1/2	cup finely chopped onion (about 1 medium)
1/4	cup water
1/2	tsp salt
1/4	tsp pepper

Sauce:

1/2	cup beef broth
1/2	cup Smoked Porter
1/4	cup apple cider vinegar
1/4	cup crushed gingersnaps (about 8)
1	Tbsp apple cider vinegar
2	Tbsp raisins

Heat oven to 400 °F.

Mix ground beef, 2/3 cup gingersnaps, onion, water, salt and pepper. Shape into 24 balls. Bake in lightly oil-sprayed pan, uncovered, for 20-25 minutes or until done and lightly browned.

Mix remaining ingredients in a large saucepan. Cook over medium heat, stirring constantly, until slightly thickened. Add raisins and meatballs and simmer until heated through. Serve with mashed potatoes or noodles. Serves 6.

Bamberg Stuffed Onions

From: Schlenkerla Brewery
Bamberg, Germany

This is a savory and authentic main event—rich, filling, and very hearty.

4 large white or yellow onions
1 Tbsp butter
1/4 tsp salt
1/2 lb. ground pork
1/4 lb. smoked pork chop, finely chopped
4 slices bread, cubed
3 eggs, lightly beaten
1/2 tsp ground pepper
1/2 tsp mace
1/2 tsp ground thyme
1/4 cup parsley, chopped
4 slices smoked bacon, cooked until crisp
2 tsp flour
1 Tbsp Maggi® or Kitchen Bouquet® seasoning
1 cup smoked beer

Heat oven to 450 °F. Cut 1/4-1/2 inch off the root end of the onion. Scoop out the center of the onion to 1/4 inch from edge. Chop removed onion and set aside.

Melt butter with salt in medium casserole.

Mix ground pork, smoked pork chop, and chopped onions. Add bread, eggs, spices, and parsley. Mix well and divide among the four hollow onions. Add a crisp bacon strip to the top of each onion and place in casserole. Bake at 450 °F for 35 minutes or until meat thermometer inserted in the largest onion reaches an internal temperature of 170 °F. Remove onions from casserole and set aside.

Scrape pan and pour drippings into a skillet over medium heat. Add Maggi or Kitchen Bouquet and flour to form a paste. Stirring constantly, slowly add all of the smoked beer until the gravy is thickened. Spoon gravy over onions and serve immediately with mashed potatoes. Serves 4.

Alaskan Smoked Porter Cheesecake

From: Alaskan Brewing Company
Juneau, Alaska
Created by Kristi Monroe, Public Relations Director

This is a dessert to die for! Not only is it beautiful to look at, but too delectable to even describe. You have to experience it yourself.

24 oz. cream cheese, room temperature
3/4 cup granulated sugar
3/4 cup light brown sugar
1 1/2 tsp salt
1 Tbsp pure vanilla
6 eggs, room temperature
2 pints sour cream, room temperature
1/3 cup cornstarch

3	cups (1 1/2 16 oz. bottles) Smoked Porter
1	cup shortbread cookie crumbs

Preheat oven to 350 °F. Boil beer until reduced to 3/4 cup. Set aside to cool. Combine cream cheese and both sugars, and mix well. Add salt, vanilla, and eggs—one at a time—beating until mixture is smooth. Blend in the sour cream, cornstarch, and reduced beer.

Press cookie crumbs into bottom of a lightly buttered springform pan. Very carefully pour in the batter and smooth until level. Put in oven, and place a pan of water on the rack below. Bake 1 hour and 45 minutes, or until center is set but still jiggles. Remove and cool overnight in the refrigerator. Serve chilled with fresh raspberries.

Smoked Porter Ginger Cake

From: Alaskan Brewing Company
Juneau, Alaska
Courtesy of Ken and MaryAnn Vaughan

This sublime and unusual cake is not baked in the oven. It's steamed on the stove, and well worth the time it takes to prepare. Porters are often paired with chocolate, but here it adds its creamy richness to a delectable cake laced with candied ginger. Once you have tasted it, your sweet palate will never be the same.

2/3	cup butter
1 1/2	cups brown sugar
3	eggs
2 1/2	cups flour
1 1/2	tsp baking powder
1/4	tsp baking soda
2	tsp ground ginger
1	tsp cinnamon

1/4	tsp nutmeg
12	oz smoked porter
1	cup candied ginger, chopped
1	cup walnuts, chopped (optional)
1	cup golden raisins

You will need a large pot, and a cake pan. Because this is actually a steamed pudding, a pudding mold is ideal. A Bundt pan, or large coffee can that will fit inside the pot are also fine. Fill the pot to about 1/3 with boiling water and simmer over low heat. Butter and flour the cake pan.

In a large mixing bowl, cream the butter and sugar until light and fluffy. Add the eggs, beating one at a time. In a separate bowl, sift together the flour and dry ingredients. Stir the flour mixture by thirds into the butter mixture, alternating with the Smoked Porter. Gently fold in the candied ginger, walnuts, and raisins, and pour into the cake pan.

Seal the top tightly with a lid or foil. If you are using a Bundt pan, poke a hole in the foil and tighten it around the tube so the steam doesn't escape into the cake.

Place the pan into the water bath. The water should come to about 1/3 up the side of the pan. Cover the entire pot and cake pan loosely with a lid or foil, and cook over low heat with the water simmering. Check occasionally to make sure the water has not evaporated. Cook 1 1/2 hours, and carefully test the cake with a sharp knife. It should come out clean. If not, replace the cover and continue to steam.

Remove the cake from the water bath and cool for 15 minutes. Loosen by running a knife around the edge of the cake. Invert on plate and lift pan from cake. Serve warm or cold with Alaskan Porter Dessert Sauce and whipped cream. Serves 8-12.

Alaskan Smoked Porter Dessert Sauce

Courtesy of Tony Hand, Distribution Coordinator
Alaskan Brewing Company

1	cup sugar
1/2	cup smoked porter
1/2	tsp crushed coriander
1/8	tsp cinnamon

In a saucepan over medium heat, stir together the sugar and porter. Add the spices and bring the mixture to a boil while stirring. Reduce heat to low and skim the foam off the top. Continue to stir and de-foam for 10 minutes.

The sauce is finished when no foam appears, and when two drops from a spoon merge as they pour. Remove from heat, cool, and serve. Wonderful over ice cream, too.

List of Smoked Beers and Their Breweries

Brewery:	**Alameda Brewing Co.**
Brewer:	Craig Nicholls
Location:	Portland, OR
Phone:	503-460-9025
Web Site:	
Name of Beer:	Croft-an-Right Wee Heavy Scottish
Style:	Wee-Heavy Scotch Ale
Smoked Malt Source:	
Wood Type:	Peat

Brewery:	**Alaskan Brewing and Bottling Co.**
Brewer:	Dayton Canaday
Location:	Juneau, AK
Phone:	907-780-5866
Web Site:	alaskanbeer.com
Name of Beer:	Alaskan Smoked Porter
Style:	Porter

Smoked Malt Source:	In House - smokehouse
Wood Type:	Alder
Brewery:	**Arcadia Brewing Co.**
Brewer:	George Murphy
Location:	Battle Creek, MI
Phone:	616-963-9520
Web Site:	arcadiabrewingcompany.com
Name of Beer:	Arcadia London Porter
Style:	Robust Porter
Smoked Malt Source:	Weyermann
Wood Type:	Beech
Brewery:	**Baltimore Brewing Co.**
Brewer:	Theo DeGroen
Location:	Baltimore, MD
Phone:	410-887-5000
Web Site:	DeGroens.com
Name of Beer:	DeGroen's Rauchbock
Style:	Rauchbock
Smoked Malt Source:	Weyermann
Wood Type:	Beech
Brewery:	**Bluegrass Brewing Co.**
Brewer:	David Pierce
Location:	Louisville, KY
Phone:	502-899-7070
Web Site:	
Name of Beer:	
Style:	Scotch Ale
Smoked Malt Source:	Weyermann
Wood Type:	Beech
Brewery:	**Boston Beer Co.**
Brewer:	Dave Grinnell
Location:	Boston, MA
Phone:	617-368-5000
Web Site:	
Name of Beer:	Sam Adams Scotch Ale
Style:	Scotch Ale

Smoked Malt Source:
Wood Type: Peat

Brewery: **Brewer's Alley**
Brewer: Tom Flores
Location: Frederick, MD
Phone: 301-631-0089
Web Site:
Name of Beer: Smoked Porter
Style: porter
Smoked Malt Source:
Wood Type: Beech

Brewery: **Brewmoon Restaurant & Micro**
Brewer: Scott Hutchinson
Location: Boston, MA
Phone: 781-707-2220
Web Site: brewmoon.com
Name of Beer: Kiawe Smoked Fest
Style: Octoberfest
Smoked Malt Source: In House - smoker
Wood Type: Kiawe (Hawaiian) & applewood
Name of Beer: Ignitor
Style: Bock
Smoked Malt Source: In House - smoker
Wood Type: Kiawe (Hawaiian) & applewood
Name of Beer: Kiawe Smoked Lager
Style: Schwarzbier
Smoked Malt Source: In House - smoker
Wood Type: Kiawe (Hawaiian) & applewood

Brewery: **Calhoun's Tennessee Microbrewery**
Brewer: Marty Velas
Location: Knoxville, TN
Phone: 423-673-337
Web Site:
Name of Beer: Kilt Tilter Scottish Ale
Style: Amber ale
Smoked Malt Source:
Wood Type:

Brewery:	**Colorado Belle**
Brewer:	Steve Peterson
Location:	Laughlin, NV
Phone:	702-298-4000
Web Site:	coloradobelle.com
Name of Beer:	Smoke Stack Lager
Style:	lager
Smoked Malt Source:	Weyermann
Wood Type:	Beech

Brewery:	**Commonwealth Brewing Co.**
Brewer:	Tod Mott
Location:	Boston, MA
Phone:	617-523-8383
Web Site:	
Name of Beer:	Smoked Dunkleweizen
Style:	Dunkleweizen
Smoked Malt Source:	
Wood Type:	

Brewery:	**Empire Brewing Co. of Syracuse**
Brewer:	Steve Schmidt
Location:	Syracuse, NY
Phone:	315-475-4409
Web Site:	empirebrewco.com
Name of Beer:	Smokin' Ale
Style:	Rauch
Smoked Malt Source:	Weyermann
Wood Type:	Beech

Brewery:	**Flat Branch Pub & Brewing Co.**
Brewer:	Marty Galloway
Location:	Columbia, MO
Phone:	573-499-0400
Web Site:	flatbranch.com
Name of Beer:	Flat Branch Smoked Porter
Style:	robust porter
Smoked Malt Source:	Bairds
Wood Type:	Peat

Name of Beer:	Flat Branch Scottish Ale
Style:	scottish ale
Smoked Malt Source:	Bairds
Wood Type:	Peat
Name of Beer:	Flat Branch Northwind Ale
Style:	heavy scottish
Smoked Malt Source:	Bairds
Wood Type:	Peat

Brewery:	**Fleetside Pub & Brewery**
Brewer:	Jim Weatherwax
Location:	Greeley, CO
Phone:	
Web Site:	
Name of Beer:	Prairie Fire Rauch
Style:	bock
Smoked Malt Source:	
Wood Type:	Hickory

Brewery:	**Flying Pig Brewing Co.**
Brewer:	Paul Scott
Location:	Everett, WA
Phone:	425-339-1393
Web Site:	
Name of Beer:	In a Pig's Eye Smoked Porter
Style:	Porter
Smoked Malt Source:	
Wood Type:	

Brewery:	**Fordham Brewing Co.**
Brewer:	Allen Young
Location:	Annapolis, MD
Phone:	410-268-4545
Web Site:	
Name of Beer:	St. John's Islay Ale
Style:	
Smoked Malt Source:	
Wood Type:	Peat

Brewery:	**Great Basin Brewing Co.**
Brewer:	Eric McClary
Location:	Sparks, NV
Phone:	775-355-7711
Web Site:	
Name of Beer:	Trail's End Smoked Chipotle Porter
Style:	porter
Smoked Malt Source:	In House - bbq pit
Wood Type:	apple & mountain mahogany
Name of Beer:	Smokejumper's Marzen
Style:	Marzen
Smoked Malt Source:	In House - bbq pit
Wood Type:	Apple & mountain mahogany

Brewery:	**H.C. Berger**
Brewer:	Patrick Dobolek
Location:	Ft. Collins, CO
Phone:	970-493-9044
Web Site:	hcberger.com
Name of Beer:	Rauch
Style:	
Smoked Malt Source:	
Wood Type:	

Brewery:	**Iron Hill Brewery**
Brewer:	Brian Finn
Location:	Newark, DE
Phone:	302-266-9000
Web Site:	
Name of Beer:	Iron Hill Wee Heavy
Style:	wee heavy
Smoked Malt Source:	
Wood Type:	Peat

Brewery:	**J.T. Garrison Brewing Co.**
Brewer:	Jay Garrison
Location:	Gardena, CA
Phone:	
Web Site:	
Name of Beer:	Scurvy Dog Grog

Style:	ale
Smoked Malt Source:	
Wood Type:	

Brewery:	**J.T. Whitney's Pub & Brewery**
Brewer:	Rich Becker
Location:	Madison, WI
Phone:	608-274-1776
Web Site:	jtwhitneys.com
Name of Beer:	Rich's Rauch Bier
Style:	Marzen
Smoked Malt Source:	Weyermann
Wood Type:	Beech

Brewery:	**John Harvard's Brew House**
Brewer:	Chris Rafferty
Location:	Wayne, PA
Phone:	610-687-6565
Web Site:	
Name of Beer:	Georgia Smoke
Style:	
Smoked Malt Source:	Weyermann
Wood Type:	Beech

Brewery:	**John Harvard's Brew House**
Brewer:	Tim Morse
Location:	Boston, MA
Phone:	617-536-7625
Web Site:	
Name of Beer:	Buckhead Smoked Weizenbock
Style:	
Smoked Malt Source:	Weyermann
Wood Type:	Beech

Brewery:	**Kegs - Alamogordo Brewing**
Brewer:	Matt Long
Location:	Alamogordo, NM
Phone:	505-434-1540
Web Site:	
Name of Beer:	Smoked Porter

Style:	porter
Smoked Malt Source:	
Wood Type:	

Brewery:	**Lafayette Brewing Co.**
Brewer:	Greg Emig
Location:	Lafayette, IN
Phone:	765-742-2591
Web Site:	
Name of Beer:	Smokehouse Porter
Style:	porter
Smoked Malt Source:	
Wood Type:	Peat

Brewery:	**Little Apple Brewing Co.**
Brewer:	Louis Kaylor
Location:	Manhattan, KS
Phone:	913-539-5500
Web Site:	
Name of Beer:	Holy Smoke!
Style:	porter
Smoked Malt Source:	
Wood Type:	

Brewery:	**Mad River Brewing Co.**
Brewer:	Tom Worley
Location:	Blue Lake, CA
Phone:	707-668-4151
Web Site:	www.madriverbrewing.com
Name of Beer:	Rock Bock
Style:	rauch bock
Smoked Malt Source:	smoke flavor extract
Wood Type:	Hickory
Name of Beer:	Steelhead Scotch Porter
Style:	scotch style porter
Smoked Malt Source:	Weyermann & Bairds
Wood Type:	Beech & peat

Brewery:	**Moose's Tooth**
Brewer:	Jimmy Butchart

Location:	Anchorage, AK
Phone:	907-270-4999
Web Site:	
Name of Beer:	Smoked Amber Ale
Style:	Amber ale
Smoked Malt Source:	in house - smoker
Wood Type:	Alder and apple

Brewery:	**Mt. Hood Brewing Co.**
Brewer:	Jon Graber
Location:	Government Camp, OR
Phone:	503-272-0102
Web Site:	
Name of Beer:	Pittock Wee Heavy Scotch Ale
Style:	winter warmer
Smoked Malt Source:	
Wood Type:	Peat

Brewery:	**Newport Beach Brewing Co.**
Brewer:	Julius Hummer
Location:	Newport Beach, CA
Phone:	714-675-8449
Web Site:	
Name of Beer:	Wee Heavy Scotch Ale
Style:	wee heavy scotch ale
Smoked Malt Source:	
Wood Type:	Peat

Brewery:	**Oregon Ale & Beer Co.**
Brewer:	Gregg LeBlanc
Location:	Oswego, OR
Phone:	503-697-8765
Web Site:	
Name of Beer:	Oregon Smoked Octoberfest
Style:	
Smoked Malt Source:	
Wood Type:	

Brewery:	**Otter Creek Brewing Co.**
Brewer:	Tom Brande

Location:	Middlebury, VT
Phone:	802-388-0727
Web Site:	ottercreekbrewing.com
Name of Beer:	Hickory Switch Smoked Amber Ale
Style:	amber ale
Smoked Malt Source:	in house
Wood Type:	Hickory

Brewery:	**Phantom Canyon Brewing Co.**
Brewer:	Erik Jefferts
Location:	Colorado Springs, CO
Phone:	719-635-2800
Web Site:	
Name of Beer:	Zebulon's Peated Porter
Style:	porter
Smoked Malt Source:	
Wood Type:	

Brewery:	**Pike Brewing Co.**
Brewer:	Kim Brusco
Location:	Seattle, WA
Phone:	206-622-3373
Web Site:	merchantduvin.com
Name of Beer:	Pike Rauchbier
Style:	
Smoked Malt Source:	
Wood Type:	

Brewery:	**Redfish New Orleans Brewhouse**
Brewer:	David Zuckerman
Location:	Boulder, CO
Phone:	303-440-5858
Web Site:	redfishbrew.com
Name of Beer:	Pelican Smoked Porter
Style:	porter
Smoked Malt Source:	Weyermann
Wood Type:	Beech

Brewery:	**RedRock Brewing Co.**
Brewer:	Eric Dunlap
Location:	Salt Lake City, UT
Phone:	801-521-7446
Web Site:	
Name of Beer:	Smoked Irish Ale
Style:	
Smoked Malt Source:	
Wood Type:	Peat

Brewery:	**Rogue Ales**
Brewer:	John Maier
Location:	Newport, OR
Phone:	541-867-3660
Web Site:	rogue.com
Name of Beer:	Incinerator doppelbock
Style:	doppelbock
Smoked Malt Source:	in house & Weyermann
Wood Type:	Beech & alder
Name of Beer:	Smoke
Style:	lager
Smoked Malt Source:	in house & Weyermann
Wood Type:	Beech & alder

Brewery:	**Stone Brewing Co.**
Brewer:	Steve Wagner
Location:	San Marcos, CA
Phone:	619-471-4999
Web Site:	www.stonebrew.com
Name of Beer:	Stone Smoked Porter
Style:	porter
Smoked Malt Source:	Bairds
Wood Type:	Peat

Brewery:	**Sweetwater Tavern & Brewery**
Brewer:	Nick Funnell
Location:	Falls Church, VA
Phone:	703-449-1100

Web Site:	
Name of Beer:	Chipotle Porter
Style:	porter
Smoked Malt Source:	in house - smokehouse
Wood Type:	Mesquite

Brewery:	**Sweetwater Tavern & Brewery**
Brewer:	Kevin McNerney
Location:	Atlanta, GA
Phone:	404-691-2537
Web Site:	
Name of Beer:	Chipotle Porter
Style:	
Smoked Malt Source:	
Wood Type:	

Brewery:	**Three Needs**
Brewer:	Glenn Walter
Location:	Burlington, VT
Phone:	802-658-0889
Web Site:	
Name of Beer:	Schwarzbier
Style:	black lager
Smoked Malt Source:	Weyermann
Wood Type:	Beech

Brewery:	**Troy Brewing Co.**
Brewer:	Peter Martin
Location:	Troy, NY
Phone:	518-273-2337
Web Site:	
Name of Beer:	Smoked Bock
Style:	bock
Smoked Malt Source:	
Wood Type:	

Brewery:	**Vermont Pub & Brewery**
Brewer:	Greg Noonan
Location:	Burlington, VT

Phone:	802-865-0500
Web Site:	vermontbrewery.com
Name of Beer:	Vermont Smoked Porter
Style:	porter
Smoked Malt Source:	In House
Wood Type:	Apple, maple, & hickory

Brewery:	**Virginia Beverage Company**
Brewer:	Alan Andrew Beal
Location:	Alexandria, VA
Phone:	703684-5397
Web Site:	
Name of Beer:	VBC Smoked Beer
Style:	
Smoked Malt Source:	
Wood Type:	

Brewery:	**Watson Brothers Brewhouse**
Brewer:	Jim Strelau
Location:	Cincinnati, OH
Phone:	513-563-9797
Web Site:	
Name of Beer:	Watson's Smoked Porter
Style:	porter
Smoked Malt Source:	Weyermann
Wood Type:	Beech

Brewery:	**Westwood Brewing Co.**
Brewer:	Ben Madden
Location:	Westwood, CA
Phone:	310-824-2739
Web Site:	
Name of Beer:	Smoked Scottish Ale
Style:	scottish ale
Smoked Malt Source:	
Wood Type:	Peat

APPENDIX C

Suppliers of Woods for Smoking

Char-Broil Grill Loverís Catalog
PO Box 1300
Columbus, GA 31902
800-242-7265
www.grilllovers.com
Hickory, Mesquite, Pecan, Oak

Charcoal Companion
7955 Edgewater Drive
Oakland, CA 94621
800-521-0505

www.companion-group.com
Wholesale only: Apple, Hickory, Mesquite, Cabernet Grape Vine

Chigger Creek Products
409 East Second Street
Sedalia, MO 65301
888-826-0702
Pecan, Mesquite, Hickory, Sassafras

Lazzari Fuel Co.
PO Box 34051
San Francisco, CA 94134
www.lazzarifuel.com
Walnut, Pecan, Apple, Alder, Maple, Oak, Cherry, Almond, Mesquire

Luhr Jensen and Sons, Inc.
PO Box 297
Hood Rive, OR 97031
800-535-1711
www.luhrjensen.com
Wholesale, but sell retail through their customer service department.
Alder, Hickory, Cherry, Mesquite, Apple.

Note that they use a small amount of alder in all of their wood blends.

APPENDIX D

Unit Conversion Chart

Index	lb. to kg	oz. to g	fl. oz. to ml
0.25	0.11	7	7
0.50	0.23	14	15
0.75	0.34	21	22
1.00	0.45	28	30
1.25	0.57	35	37
1.50	0.68	43	44
1.75	0.79	50	52
2.00	0.91	57	59
2.25	1.02	64	67
2.50	1.13	71	74
2.75	1.25	78	81
3.00	1.36	85	89
3.25	1.47	92	96
3.50	1.59	99	103
3.75	1.70	106	111
4.00	1.81	113	118
4.25	1.93	120	126
4.50	2.04	128	133
4.75	2.15	135	140
5.00	2.27	142	148
5.25	2.38	149	155
5.50	2.49	156	163
5.75	2.61	163	170
6.00	2.72	170	177
6.25	2.84	177	185
6.50	2.95	184	192
6.75	3.06	191	200
7.00	3.18	198	207
7.25	3.29	206	214
7.50	3.40	213	222
7.75	3.52	220	229
8.00	3.63	227	237
8.25	3.74	234	244
8.50	3.86	241	251
8.75	3.97	248	259
9.00	4.08	255	266
9.25	4.20	262	274
9.50	4.31	269	281
9.75	4.42	276	288
10.00	4.54	283	296
10.25	4.65	291	303
10.50	4.76	298	310
10.75	4.88	305	318
11.00	4.99	312	325
11.25	5.10	319	333
11.50	5.22	326	340
11.75	5.33	333	347
12.00	5.44	340	355

By Philip W. Fleming and Joachim Schüring. Reprinted with permission from *Zymurgy*®.

gal. to l		qt. to l		pt. to l		tsp.	tbsp.	cup
US	UK	US	UK	US	UK	to ml	to ml	to ml
0.95	1.14	0.24	0.28	0.12	0.14	1.2	3.7	59
1.89	2.27	0.47	0.57	0.24	0.28	2.5	7.4	118
2.84	3.41	0.71	0.85	0.35	0.43	3.7	11.1	177
3.79	4.55	0.95	1.14	0.47	0.57	4.9	14.8	237
4.73	5.68	1.18	1.42	0.59	0.71	6.2	18.5	296
5.68	6.82	1.42	1.70	0.71	0.85	7.4	22.2	355
6.62	7.96	1.66	1.99	0.83	0.99	8.6	25.9	414
7.57	9.09	1.89	2.27	0.95	1.14	9.9	29.6	473
8.52	10.23	2.13	2.56	1.06	1.28	11.1	33.3	532
9.46	11.36	2.37	2.84	1.18	1.42	12.3	37.0	591
10.41	12.50	2.60	3.13	1.30	1.56	13.6	40.2	651
11.36	13.64	2.84	3.41	1.42	1.70	14.8	44.4	710
12.30	14.77	3.08	3.69	1.54	1.85	16.0	48.1	769
13.25	15.91	3.31	3.98	1.66	1.99	17.3	51.8	828
14.19	17.05	3.55	4.26	1.77	2.13	18.5	55.4	887
15.14	18.18	3.79	4.55	1.89	2.27	19.7	59.1	946
16.09	19.32	4.02	4.83	2.01	2.42	20.9	62.8	1,005
17.03	20.46	4.26	5.11	2.13	2.56	22.2	66.5	1,065
17.98	21.59	4.50	5.40	2.25	2.70	23.4	70.2	1,124
18.93	22.73	4.73	5.68	2.37	2.84	24.6	73.9	1,183
19.87	23.87	4.97	5.97	2.48	2.98	25.9	77.6	1,242
20.82	25.00	5.20	6.25	2.60	3.13	27.1	81.3	1,301
21.77	26.14	5.44	6.53	2.72	3.27	28.3	85.0	1,360
22.71	27.28	5.68	6.82	2.84	3.41	29.6	88.7	1,419
23.66	28.41	5.91	7.10	2.96	3.55	30.8	92.4	1,479
24.60	29.55	6.15	7.39	3.08	3.69	32.0	96.1	1,538
25.55	30.69	6.39	7.67	3.19	3.84	33.3	99.8	1,597
26.50	31.82	6.62	7.96	3.31	3.98	34.5	103.5	1,656
27.44	32.96	6.86	8.24	3.43	4.12	35.7	107.2	1,715
28.39	34.09	7.10	8.52	3.55	4.26	37.0	110.9	1,774
29.34	35.23	7.33	8.81	3.67	4.40	38.2	114.6	1,834
30.28	36.37	7.57	9.09	3.79	4.55	39.4	118.3	1,893
31.23	37.50	7.81	9.38	3.90	4.69	40.7	122.0	1,952
32.18	38.64	8.04	9.66	4.02	4.83	41.9	125.7	2,011
33.12	39.78	8.28	9.94	4.14	4.97	43.1	129.4	2,070
34.07	40.91	8.52	10.23	4.26	5.11	44.4	133.1	2,129
35.01	42.05	8.75	10.51	4.38	5.26	45.6	136.8	2,188
36.96	43.19	9.99	10.80	4.50	5.40	46.8	140.5	2,248
37.91	44.32	9.23	11.08	4.61	5.54	48.1	144.2	2,307
37.85	45.46	9.46	11.36	4.73	5.68	49.3	147.9	2,366
38.80	46.60	9.70	11.65	4.85	5.82	50.5	151.6	2,425
39.75	47.73	9.94	11.93	4.97	5.97	51.8	155.3	2,484
40.69	48.87	10.17	12.22	5.09	6.11	53.0	159.0	2,543
41.64	50.01	10.41	12.50	5.20	6.25	54.2	162.6	2,602
42.58	51.14	10.65	12.79	5.32	6.39	55.4	166.3	2,662
43.53	52.28	10.88	13.07	5.44	6.53	56.7	170.0	2,721
44.48	53.41	11.12	13.35	5.56	6.68	57.9	173.7	2,780
45.42	54.55	11.36	13.64	5.68	6.82	59.1	177.4	2,839

Glossary

adjunct. Any unmalted grain or other fermentable ingredient added to the mash.

aeration. The action of introducing air to the wort at various stages of the brewing process. Proper aeration before primary fermentation is vital to a vigorous ferment.

airlock. *See* **fermentation** lock.

airspace. *See* **ullage.**

alcohol by volume (v/v). The percentage of volume of alcohol per volume of beer. To calculate the approximate volumetric alcohol content, subtract the final gravity from the original gravity and divide the result by 0.0075. For example: 1.050 – 1.012 = 0.038 ÷ 0.0075 = 5% v/v.

alcohol by weight (w/v). The percentage weight of alcohol per volume of beer. To calculate the approximate alcohol content by weight, subtract the final gravity from the original gravity and multiply by 105. For example: 1.050 – 1.0212 = 0.038 x 105 = 4% w/v.

ale. 1. Historically, an unhopped malt beverage. 2. Now, a generic term for hopped beers produced by top fermentation, as opposed to lagers, which are produced by bottom fermentation.

all-extract beer. A beer made with only malt extract as opposed to one made from barley or a combination of malt extract and barley.

Glossary

all-grain beer. A beer made with only malted barley as opposed to one made from malt extract or from malt extract and malted barley.

all-malt beer. A beer made with only barley malt with no adjuncts nor refined sugars.

alpha acid. A soft resin in hop cones. When boiled, alpha acids are converted to iso-alpha-acids, which account for 60 percent of a beer's bitterness.

alpha-acid unit. A measurement of the potential bitterness of hops, expressed by their percentage of alpha acid. Low is 2–4 percent; medium is 5–7 percent; high is 8–12 percent. Abbreviation is AAU.

attenuation. The reduction in the wort's specific gravity caused by the transformation of sugars into alcohol and carbon dioxide.

autolysis. A process in which yeast feed on each other, producing a rubbery odor. To avoid this, rack beer to remove excess yeast as soon after fermentation as possible.

Bitterness Units (BU). A measurement of the American Society for Brewing Chemists for bittering substances in beer, primarily iso-alpha-acids, but also including oxidized beta acids. *See* **also International Bitterness Units.**

blow-by (blow-off). A single-stage homebrewing fermentation method in which a plastic tube is fitted into the mouth of a carboy, and the other end is submerged in a pail of sterile water. Unwanted residues and carbon dioxide are expelled through the tube, while air is prevented from coming into contact with the fermenting beer, thus avoiding contamination.

carbonation. The process of introducing carbon dioxide into a liquid by: (1) injecting the finished beer with carbon dioxide; (2) adding young fermenting beer to finished beer for a renewed fermentation (kraeusening); (3) priming (adding sugar) to fermented wort prior to bottling, creating a secondary fermentation in the bottle.

carboy. A large glass, plastic, or earthenware bottle.

chalk (calcium carbonate). Often added to sparge water to achieve a more efficient extraction of sugars.

chill haze. Haziness caused by protein and tannin during the secondary fermentation.

cold break. The flocculation of proteins and tannins during wort cooling.

decoction. A method of mashing that raises the temperature of the wash by removing a portion, boiling it, and returning it to the mash tun.

diacetyl. A strong aromatic compound in beer that adds a butterlike flavor.

dimethyl sulfide (DMS). A major sulfur compound of lagers. DMS is released during boiling as a gas that dissipates into the atmosphere.

dry-hopping. The addition of hops to the primary fermenter, the secondary fermenter, or to casked beer to add aroma and hop character to the finished beer without adding significant bitterness.

dry malt. Malt extract in powdered form.

European Brewery Convention (EBC). *See* **Standard Reference Method.**

esters. A group of compounds in beer, which impart fruity flavors.

extract. The amount of dissolved materials in the wort after mashing and lautering malted barley and/or malt adjuncts such as corn and rice.

fermentation lock. A one-way valve, which allows carbon dioxide to escape from the fermenter while excluding contaminants.

final gravity. The specific gravity of a beer when fermentation is complete.

fining. The process of adding clarifying agents to beer during secondary fermentation to precipitate suspended matter.

flocculant yeast. Yeast cells that form large colonies and tend to come out of suspension before the end of fermentation.

flocculation. The behavior of yeast cells joining into masses and settling out toward the end of fermentation.

fusel alcohol. High molecular weight alcohol, which results from excessively high fermentation temperatures. Fusel alcohol can impart harsh bitter flavors to beer as well as contribute to hangovers.

gelatin. A fining agent added during secondary fermentation, clarifying the beer.

Homebrew Bittering Units. A formula invented by the American Homebrewers Association to measure bitterness of beer. Calculate bittering units by multiplying the percent alpha acid in the hops by the number of ounces. Example: if 1.5 ounces of 10 percent alpha acid hops were used in a 5-gallon batch, the total homebrew bittering units would be 15:

1.5 x 10 = 15 HBU per 5 gallons.

hop pellets. Finely powdered hop cones compressed into tablets. Hop pellets are 20–30 percent more bitter by weight than the same variety in loose form.

hydrometer. A glass instrument used to measure the specific gravity of liquids as compared to water, consisting of a graduated stem resting on a weighed float.

infusion mash. *See* **step infusion.**

IBU (International Bitterness Units). The measurement of the European Brewing Convention for the concentration of iso-alpha-acids in 34 milligrams per liter (parts per million) in wort and beer. *See also* **Bitterness Units.**

Irish moss. Copper or lead "finings" that help precipitate proteins in the kettle. *See also* **cold break.**

isinglass. A gelatinous substance made from the swim bladder of certain fish and added to beer as a fining agent.

kellerbier. Unfiltered lager beer that is often carbonated by secondary. fermentation in the serving vessel.

kraeusen. The rocky head of foam which appears on the surface of the wort during fermentation. v.. To add fermenting wort to fermented beer to induce carbonation through a secondary fermentation.

lager. A generic term for any bottom-fermented beer. Lager brewing is now the predominant brewing method worldwide except in Britain where top-fermented ales dominate. v. To store beer at near-zero temperatures in order to precipitate yeast cells and proteins and improve taste.

lauter tun. A vessel in which the mash settles and the grains are removed from the sweet wort through a straining process. It has a false slotted bottom and spigot.

liquefaction. The process by which alpha-amylase enzymes degrade soluble starch into dextrin.

Lovibond (°L). The scale used to measure beer color. See also Standard Reference Method.

malt. Barley that has been steeped in water, germinated, then dried in kilns. This process converts insoluble starches to soluble substances and sugars.

malt extract. A thick syrup or dry powder prepared from malt.

mashing. Mixing crushed malt with water to extract the fermentables, degrade haze-forming proteins, and convert grain starches to fermentable sugars and nonfermentable carbohydrates.

modification. 1. The physical and chemical changes in barley as a result of malting. 2. The degree to which these changes have occurred, as determined by the growth of the acrospire.

original gravity. The specific gravity of wort previous to fermentation. A measure of the total amount of dissolved solids in wort.

pH. A measure of acidity or alkalinity of a solution, usually on a scale of 1 to 14, where 7 is neutral.

phenolic. Compounds that give a spicy character to beer, as in the hefeweizen style.

pitching. The process of adding yeast to the cooled wort.

Plato. A saccharometer that expresses specific gravity as extract weight in a 100-gram solution at 68 °F (20 °C). A revised, more accurate version of Balling, developed by Dr. Plato.

primary fermentation. The first stage of fermentation, during which most fermentable sugars are converted to ethyl alcohol and carbon dioxide.

priming sugar. A small amount of corn, malt, or cane sugar added to bulk beer prior to racking or at bottling to induce a new fermentation and create carbonation.

racking. The process of transferring beer from one container to another, especially into the final package (bottles, kegs).

recirculation. Clarifying the wort before it moves from the lauter tun into the kettle by recirculating it through the wash bed.

saccharification. The naturally occurring process in which malt starch is converted into fermentable sugars, primarily maltose.

saccharometer. An instrument that determines the sugar concentration of a solution by measuring the specific gravity.

secondary fermentation. 1. The second slower stage of fermentation, lasting from a few weeks to many months depending on the type of beer. 2. A fermentation occurring in bottles or casks and initiated by priming or by adding yeast.

sparging. Spraying the spent grains in the mash with hot water to retrieve the remaining malt sugar.

specific gravity. A measure of a substance's density as compared to that of water, which is given the value of 1.000 at 39.2 °F (4 °C). Specific gravity has no accompanying units because it is expressed as a ratio.

Standard Reference Method (SRM) and European Brewery Convention (EBC). Two different analytical methods of describing color developed by comparing color samples. Degrees SRM, approximately equivalent to degrees Lovibond, are used by the American Society of Brewing Chemists (ASBC) while degrees EBC are European units. The following equations show approximate conversions: (°EBC) = 2.65 x (°Lovibond) – 1.2 and (°Lovibond) = 0.377 x (°EBC) + 0.45.

starter. A batch of fermenting yeast, added to the wort to initiate fermentation.

step infusion. A method of mashing whereby the temperature of the mash is raised by adding very hot water, and then stirring and stabilizing the mash at the target step temperature.

strike temperature. The initial temperature of the water when the malted barley is added to it to create the mash.

torrefied wheat. Wheat which has been heated quickly at high temperature, causing it to puff up, which renders it easily mashed.

trub. Suspended particles resulting from the precipitation of proteins, hop oils, and tannins during boiling and cooling stages of brewing.

tun. Any open tank or vessel.

ullage. The empty space between a liquid and the top of its container. Also called airspace or headspace.

v/v. *See* **alcohol by volume.**

vorlauf. To recirculate the wort from one mash tun through the grain bed to clarify.

w/v. *See* **alcohol by weight**.

water hardness. The degree of dissolved minerals in water.

whirlpool. A method of bringing cold break material to the center of the kettle by stirring the wort until a vortex is formed.

wort. The mixture that results from mashing the malt and boiling the hops, before it is fermented into beer.

References

Amsinck, George Stewart. *Practical Brewings: A Series of Fifty Brewings*. London: Self-published, 1868.

Anonymous. *Vollkommene Bierbrauerei nebst Branntwein-Brennerei und Essig-Fabrikation*. Ulm: J. Ebner'schen, 1838.

Anonymous. *One Hundred Years of Brewing*. Chicago and New York: H.S. Rich and Co., 1903.

Ballard-Tremeer, Grant. *Emissions of Rural Wood-Burning Cooking Devices* [Ph.D. dissertation]. Johannesburg: University of the Witwatersrand, Faculty of Engineering, 1997.

Black, William. *A Practical Treatise on Brewing*. London: Longman, Brown, Green and Longmans, 1849.

Byrn, M.L. *The Complete Practical Brewer*. Philadelphia: Henry Carey Baird, 1860.

Corran, H.S. *A History of Brewing*. London: David and Charles, 1975.

Daniels, Ray. *Designing Great Beers*. Boulder, Colorado: Brewers Publications, 1996.

Dawson, Tim. "Smoky Beer: Brewing with Smoked Malts." *Brewing Techniques* 4, no. 3 (May/June 1996).

Ellis, William. *The London and Country Brewer* (third edition). London: T. Astley, 1737.

__________. *The London and Country Brewer* (fourth edition). London: T. Astley, 1742.

Guillen, Maria D., and Maria L. Ibargoitia. "Relationships between the Maximum Temperature Reached in the Smoke Generation Processes from *Vitis vinifera* L. Shoot Sawdust and Composition of the Aqueous Smoke Flavoring Preparations Obtained." *Journal of Agricultural and Food Chemistry* 44, 1302–1307 (1996).

_________. "New Components with Potential Antioxidant and Organoleptic Properties, Detected for the First Time in Liquid Smoke Flavoring Preparations." *Journal of Agricultural and Food Chemistry* 46, 1276–1285 (1998).

Guillen, Maria D., and Maria J. Manzanos. "Extractable Components of the Aerial Parts of *Salvia lavandulifolia* and Composition of the Liquid Smoke Flavoring Obtained from Them." *Journal of Agricultural and Food Chemistry* 47, 3016-3027 (1999).

Harrison, William. *The Description of England.* New York: Dover Publications, 1994 (Originally published 1577).

Hughes, E. A. *Treatise on the Brewing of Beer and Porter.* Uxbridge: T. Lake, 1798.

Jackson, Michael. *Michael Jackson's Beer Companion.* Philadelphia: Running Press, 1993.

King, Frank A. *Beer Has a History.* London: Fleet Street Press, 1947.

Krüniß, Johan Georg. *Oekonomische Encyklopadie of Allegemeines System* [Fifth part, from beer to flowers]. Berlin: Joachim Pauli, 1784.

Levesque, John. *The Art of Brewing and Fermenting.* London: J. Leath, 1853.

Leyser, E. *Die Bierbrauerei.* Stuttgart: Verlag von Max Waag, 1893.

Lutz, H. F. *Viticulture and Brewing in the Ancient Orient.* New York: G. E. Stechert & Company, 1922.

Maga, Joseph A. *Smoke in Food Processing.* Boca Raton: CRC Press, 1988.

Mangino, Mario M., Richard A. Scanlan, and Terrence J. O'Brien "*N*-Nitrosamines in Beer." J. American Chemical Society, 229–245 (1981).

Mathias, Peter. *The Brewing Industry in England 1700–1830.* Cambridge: University Press, 1959.

More, Sir J. *England's Interest.* London: F. Hove, 1703.

Narziss, Ludwig. "Die Entwicklung der Mälzereitechnik und technologie seit 1860." *Brauwelt* 32, 1406–1418 (1986).

Nordland, Odd. *Brewing and Beer Traditions in Norway*. Oslo: The Norwegian Research Council for Science and the Humanities, 1969.

Pigott, George M. *Smoking Fish: Special Considerations.* Seattle: University of Washington, Institute for Food Science and Technology, 1980.

Renfrow, Cindy. Personal communication quoting Markham. July 2,1998.

Richardson, John. *The Philosophical Principles of the Science of Brewing.* York: G. G. and J. Robinson, 1788.

Roberts, W.H. *The Scottish Ale Brewer and Practical Maltster* (second edition). London: Whittaker & Company, 1846.

________. *The Scottish Ale Brewer and Practical Maltster* (third edition). London: Whittaker and Company, 1847.

Schönfeld, Franz. Obergärige Biere und ihre Herstellung. Berlin: Verlag von Paul Parey, 1938.

Seifert, Johann Albert Joseph. *Das Bamberger Bier.* Bamberg: Meisenbach, 1992 (reprinted; originally published 1818).

Shafizadeh, F. "Basic Principles of Direct Combustion," in *Biomass Conversion Processes for Energy and Fuels,* S.S. Sofer and O.R. Zaborsky (eds.). New York: Plenum Publishing Corporation, 1981.

________. "Chemistry of Pyrolysis and Combustion of Wood," in *Proceedings: 1981 International Conference on Residential Solid Fuels—Environmental Impacts and Solutions,* J. A. Cooper and D. Malek (eds.). Beaverton: Oregon Graduate Center, 1982.

Simon, Johann Christian. *Die Kunst des Bierbrauens.* Dresden: Waltherischen Hofbuchhandlung, 1803.

Simonelt, Bernd R. T., W. F. Rogge, M. A. Mazurek, L. G. Standley, L. M. Hildemann, and G. R. Cass. "Lignin Pyrolysis Products, Lignins and Resin Acids as Specific Tracers of Plant Classes in Emissions from Biomass Combustion" *Environmental Science and Technology* 27:2533–2541 (1993).

Steel, James. *Selection of the Practical Points of Malting and Brewing and Strictures Thereon, For the Use of Brewery Proprietors*. Glasgow: Robert Anderson, 1878.

Stopes, H. *Malt and Malting: An Historical, Scientific and Practical Treatise*. London: F. W. Lyon, 1885.

Strong, Stanley. *The Romance of Brewing*. Privately Circulated. c.1954.

Thausing, Julius E. *Die Theorie und Praxis der Malzbereitung und Bierfabrikation*. Leipzig: I. M. Gebhardt, 1898.

Tizzard, W.L. *The Theory and Practice of Brewing Illustrated* (fourth edition). London: Self-published, 1857.

Tuck, John. *The Private Brewer's Guide to the Art of Brewing Ale and Porter*. London: W. Simpkin and R. Marshall, 1822. Reprinted, Mattituck, New York: Zymoscribe, 1995.

von Canerin, Franz Ludwig. *Abhandlung von der Anlage . . . einer vollkommen eingerichteten Bierbrauerei*. Frankfurt am Main: Hermann, 1791.

Wahl, R., and Henius, M. *The American Handy-Book of the Brewing, Malting and Auxiliary Trades*. Chicago: Wahl-Henius Institute, 1901, 1908.

White, Edward Skeate. *The Maltster's Guide*. London: W. R. Loftus.

Index

Index

Index

Index

About the Authors

Geoff Larson is founder, president, and brewmaster of Alaskan Brewing and Bottling Company in Juneau, Alaska. He and his brewery are renowned internationally for their multi-award-winning Alaskan Smoked Porter, a seasonal beer using alder-smoked malt that has helped rekindle interest in smoked beers in the United States. In 1999, the company was selected as the Small Business of the Year for the State of Alaska.

How did all this happen? Following graduation from the University of Maryland with a degree in chemical engineering, Geoff followed his true love,

Marcy, who "had stolen his heart", to Alaska. An avid homebrewer, Geoff further developed his knowledge of brewing science at Siebel Institute of Technology. In 1985, he and his wife, Marcy, founded their company.

The son of a Foreign Service Officer, he was born in Caracas, Venezuela, and spent much of his early life stationed at various embassies in South America and Europe. Summer vacations on his relative's farm in North Dakota, where he learned about harvesting and life on the farm, prepared him, he says, for his future self-sufficient, rugged lifestyle in Alaska. Now he finds special satisfaction in the wilds of Alaska, traveling from the Arctic Ocean in the far north, down to the rain-forests of Alaska's southern coastline.

Ray Daniels is an award-winning author and well-known expert on craft brewing. He has served as editor-in-chief of *Zymurgy* and *The New Brewer*, and director of Craft Beer Marketing for the Brewers Association. His writings on beer and brewing have won numerous awards from the North American Guild of Beer Writers. In 1998 he was named Beer Writer of the Year.

His many achievements include founding the Real Ale Festival, which annually presented the largest collection of British-style, cask-conditioned ales anywhere outside of Great Britain. As a brewer, he has won nearly 100 regional homebrewing awards, as well as several national accolades. Every year he judges at homebrew and commercial beer competitions, including the Great American Beer Festival, World Beer Cup, and the National Homebrew Competition.

He also knows whereof he speaks. He is a top graduate of Siebel Institute's diploma course in brewing, holds an MBA from Harvard, and earned his B.S. degree in Biochemistry from Texas A&M.

He is also author of award-winning *Designing Great Beers, 101 Ideas for Homebrew Fun*, and is coauthor of *Brown Ale*, all published by Brewers Publications.